Fun Ideas for Kids

MIMI WELLISCH

It is before they get to
school that children
are likely to do their
best learning.

John Holt, Educator

LEOPARD

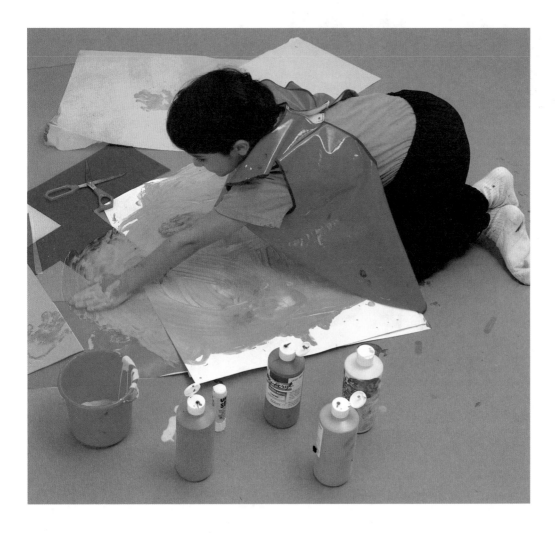

This edition published in 1995 by Leopard Books
Random House, 20 Vauxhall Bridge Road, London SW1V 2SA

First published in 1992 by Murdoch Books®, a division of Murdoch Magazines Pty Ltd

© Murdoch Books®, 1992

© Text: Mimi Wellisch 1992

ISBN 0 7529 0086 2

Designer: Lin Norman
Photographer: Peter Sledge
Illustrator: Loui Silvestro
Finished Art: Jayne Hunter
Craftmaker: Jan Hook

Typeset by Adtype, North Sydney
Produced by Mandarin Offset, Hong Kong

The Publisher would like to thank the following for the loan of props for photography: **teddy bear**, Hide 'n'
Seek, Mosman, NSW; **child's shoes**, Bonza Brats, Mosman, NSW; **bike and helmet**, Neutral Bay Cycles,
Neutral Bay, NSW; **white soup bowl**, Accoutrement, Mosman, NSW.

Acknowledgements

Thank you to publisher Anne Wilson for offering me this magnificent opportunity, and to my editor Susan Tomnay for giving me free rein.

And thank you to my mother, my late father, my stepfather and stepmother who together made my life possible.

And last but certainly not least, thank you to my children: Michelle, Vivienne, Joshua and Nicola — as well as all the little children who it was my privilege to teach, and who taught me what I know.

To all the little children and their parents who will play and gain enjoyment from the games in this book.

CONTENTS

The First Critical Years

In thinking about children, two powerful facts emerge:

- Children are a nation's greatest potential asset: in time they will become its writers, scientists, philosophers, workers, and decision-makers.
- Children are constantly learning — every second of the day. They are learning how to become adults.

Each fully expressed individual makes a valid contribution to our society, just by being who he is. So any energy and effort put into children — be it time or money — can be viewed as an investment in the future. We who have children in our care — or even those of us who deal with children *some* of the time — are well served by making it our business to find out all we can about the true nature of the child.* We can learn how best to foster his full expression, and put into practice what we know. In this way we can add to, and support, a child in achieving his full potential.

The first five years of a child's life are most important. Given the right environment during these years, a healthy child. has the ability to transform himself from a helpless and dependent infant into a capable and articulate little person. In these five years the foundations for relating, inquiry, critical thinking, and creativity — in fact, a child's entire personality — is established.

'As you observe how your child goes about exploring and experimenting, you will without a doubt realise what an amazing, capable, ingenious, curious, resourceful, and wonderful being you have brought into this world.'

This book has been written in order to assist you, the concerned and interested adult, in:

- *fostering a good relationship with the child*
- *providing the correct learning environment*
- *encouraging his innate curiosity about life*
- *creating solid educational opportunities*
- *helping the child who has a learning problem*

Throughout the text you will find a wealth of activities and ideas on how to make simple, inexpensive and effective learning materials. These suggestions are by no means exhaustive, and you are encouraged to create new ones as the need and inspiration arises.

While you and your child do the activities you may notice how much fun you are having, that you are relating in a new way with each other and how mutually beneficial it is to spend time together. As you observe how your child goes about exploring and experimenting, you will without a doubt realise what an amazing, capable, ingenious, curious, resourceful, and wonderful being you have brought into this world.

* *Throughout this book the child will be referred to as 'he' or 'she' interchangeably.*

Right: Tracing around child's body shape to make a Punching Joe (see p. 92).

4

HOW CHILDREN LEARN

Since the time of Jean Jacques Rousseau (1712–1778) educators have been aware that children learn chiefly by their own experimentation and errors. More recent findings have revealed — much to some educators' disappointment — that the process of learning is mainly developmental and cannot be hurried along; but it *is* possible to miss the optimum time for easier learning (which does not depend on the age of the child, but upon individual maturation) by denying the child opportunities he requires, or through lack of a stimulating environment.

So, for instance, although we can model walking to a baby, *he* determines when he is ready, and *he* eventually has to take his own first steps alone, risking inevitable falls. It is not possible to teach a baby how to walk, and it would be ridiculous to try. But we can afford him many opportunities for walking and objects he can pull himself up with, hang on to, and walk along, as well as cheer him on enthusiastically. In the same way we cannot place 'reading' into the mind of the child, but we can be avid readers ourselves, and read to the child, as well as provide many varied and stimulating opportunities for the child to experience which will lead him there.

Brain research has revealed that the left and the right hemispheres of the human brain have different functions. The left brain controls mainly analytical, sequential, logical and linguistic functions, while the right brain's domain is the non-verbal, spatial, visual, and creative functions.

So if you were to, say, compose a song, the words would be supplied from the left hemisphere of the brain, and the tune from the right.

It has also been found that we use only 5–10 per cent of our total brain capacity. And other research has shown that stimulating sensory environments where animals have been free to explore and experiment, have increased and changed their brain size, weight and structure.

Education of children to date has predominantly concentrated on left brain learning which produces tangible results such as reading and number skills, while the right brain learning has been given very little consideration.

It is important to implement what we know about right brain (creative) and left brain (logic) functions by offering the child opportunities to create, explore and daydream. These experiences are the foundations of basic knowledge, which the child expresses through the conscious use of language.

This book has applied up-to-date knowledge on early learning and offers a balanced variety of learning experiences.

PLAY . . . WHAT IS IT?

Play is a child's constant state of activity: whatever a child does, is play. Play is a learning child's active and creative expression. The essential and observable actions of play are:

> *Observation*
> *Imitation*
> *Exploration*
> *Experimentation*
> *Repetition*

Additionally, we know that children gather information through their five perceptual senses of:

> *Sight*
> *Hearing*
> *Taste*
> *Touch*
> *Smell*

All the activities presented here make use of the above. For instance, food (sight, hearing, taste, touch, smell) is used in pre-mathematics as a bridge to the concept of number ('How many slices of carrots, now?').

It is advocated that you demonstrate to the child (*observation*), encourage the child to try the activity (*imitation, exploration*), give the child space to *experiment* within reason, and let the child *repeat* the activity at some other time.

MISTAKES

Children learn through the process of doing, through trial and error, through experimentation and exploration. While playing, children risk making what we term 'mistakes'. Where mistakes do not occur, real learning does not take place. Unfortunately many of us have been led to believe that a mistake is a sort of failure to perform perfectly. But how many of us would be walking today if we had been mocked, shamed or humiliated for stumbling as we took our first step? We would not dream of doing that to a baby, but our expectations change as a child grows older.

People tend to fear that their child might be lazy or dumb. Going back to the metaphor of the walking baby, we all learn to walk, provided we are able. We all have an innate drive to improve ourselves, to succeed. What kills the drive in many of us is the fear of failure! If we trust our child to want to learn and to succeed, as with walking, we can allow him to make the mistakes he needs to make. Without the mistakes he cannot learn to adjust his aim, and we cannot do the falling for him. What we *can* do is to be sensitive to his needs, provide him with role models, opportunities, reasonable safety, and encouragement.

'Play is the essence of experience and knowledge.'

Children are veritable learning sponges, and uniquely adaptable — they will learn Japanese in Japan, and English in Australia. They will learn to count, read, play an instrument — they are able to learn whatever their environment affords them.

Yet equally, each child is born with his own unique personality and potential talents. He is unique because no-one else is quite like him. This is why it is so important to consider the *quality* of his actual experiences during the early childhood years: with care, he can be helped to unfurl his unique abilities through playful experimentation. And, if encouraged and stimulated — but not for the sake of results, or a far-off future — he will know himself, as well as the world, and will be equipped to choose his ways wisely, confidently, and creatively.

There is therefore a real risk in assuming what a young child needs to learn, and then teaching it relentlessly. The risk is that while we stuff him with unquestioned, undigested facts, we sweep aside and suffocate whatever real potentials he may need to develop. And we will never benefit from these, they will remain lost forever — along with the real spirit of this unique child. Such a child will learn to perform, and to please others. He will, however, not be able to trust his own judgement and will always have to rely on others for information because his learning will have been shallow, superficial, and not his own. He will not have learnt very deeply about life, and will be blind to possibilities other than his limited experiences; he will not know himself, nor therefore others.

And, of course, there is the sheer impossibility of the teaching task: not only is it a joyless way of teaching and learning, but no matter how early we may head start to cram a child, it will not be possible to keep updating the ever-changing 'facts'.

The key is to kindle a *thinking* child; guide him towards the discovery of useful information; and allow him — with respect — to take the credit for his discoveries, as well as discussing with him what he has found, and tantalising his mind with related matters which may interest him.

A thinking child is one who speaks a lot, asks a lot of questions, is often heard, and receives encouraging responses. It is not difficult to bring up such a child. You can create a positive learning environment for your child, and enjoy it, together.

'In the early years, facts and feelings are not clearly differentiated — and feelings endure longer than facts, at any age. There is a much greater chance that a fact will take root in the mind if it comes in on the wings of a feeling, a stirring of the emotions was well as the intellect.'

Dorothy Butler, Children's Literature expert

'The parent must never forget that learning is life's most exciting game — it is not work.'

Glen Doman, Author of 'Teach Your Baby To Read'

PROCESS OR PRODUCT

Adults want to see *results*. Learning children need to experience *process*. This is an important point to understand if you want to have a child succeed. If you worry about how the child's work looks, she will eventually stop trying. After all, she can't do it as well as you, she cannot compete.

The child lives in the present, totally absorbed. Every action is a trying-out of a new skill. For this reason, the act of *attempting* must be seen as the end product in the work of a child. If she writes her name with letters all over the place, the admirable thing is how well she has tried something new, not how it looks as a finished product to an adult's critical eye. Children put a lot of effort into their work, as you will discover.

Trust that the child has an inner drive to keep repeating over and over again naturally until she masters the skill. All you need to do is to encourage her as she refines her skills. However, if a child balks at a particular activity, give it a rest for a while. Chances are that she has reached a learning plateau and satiated herself in that area. She will probably want to return to it later with added zest and with a more integrated attitude and ability.

Another difference between adult and child is with relationship to time. Results have a time limit, while process is always in the now. Small children experience a constant time: the present. You are encouraged to enter this timeless zone with your child while you work together. Avoid hurrying the child, forget what you need to do later. Be fully present with your child and her actions during your short (morning) session. Today's adults would all benefit by learning again the joy of living fully in the present from children. Here is your opportunity to re-enter the timeless zone of *play*.

DISCIPLINE AND LIMITS

You may wonder what discipline has to do with learning. How you discipline your child is part and parcel of her learning experiences and environment. Although *you* may perceive changes in your role from teacher (working with her on the activities in this book) to mother (tucking her into bed), her role as a learning child remains constant. Therefore the form of discipline she experiences in all situations ought to be consistent — and eventually predictable — in all her daily experiences. So how you set your limits, and what you will allow, affect both your child's attitude to learning and the opportunities that are available to her.

Discipline is a contentious issue. Teachers spend a lot of time on this subject during school hours. There are about as many opinions on how to discipline children as there are people. Obviously, your own upbringing will influence the way you prefer to discipline your child.

There seem to be three main kinds of parenting styles, and there is research available which indicates that one of those parenting styles is more effective than the others:

Authoritarian parenting is the conservative mode — it requires unquestioning obedience of the child. A child brought up in this manner displays more discon-

- *Look at what lay behind the undesirable action*
- *Look at the problem, not the person*
- *Do not offer choice if there are no choices*
- *Be firm — do not change your decisions*
- *Never argue with your child*
- *Do not delay action if action is necessary*
- *Do not punish yourself with the action chosen (will you or your child suffer more if he misses out on dessert?). Choose action thoughtfully.*
- *Is the action you have chosen reasonable when considering the unwanted behaviour?*
- *Do not feel guilty if you have made a mistake — mistakes are learning opportunities, remember?*
- *Explain your action, but do not justify it.*
- *Do not expect immediate results, remember that children learn by repetition.*

> 'To help our children . . . we must turn . . . to a new order based on the principles of freedom and responsibility.'
>
> *Dr. R. Dreikurs, M.D. and Author*

tented behaviour, and is more withdrawn and distrustful than other children, according to a study on preschoolers.

Permissive parenting requires little of the child — it allows the child to be self-regulating, on the whole. A child brought up in this way displays, surprisingly, less maturity and self-reliance, and is also less keen to explore, than are children disciplined in other ways.

Directional parenting acknowledges the child's expressed needs and, although rules are firm, there is a willingness to listen to the child's point of view and to give and take. These children are self-reliant, exploratory, and content.

Helpful hints on directional parenting:

- *Be consistent*
- *Consider your child's actual level of understanding*
- *Consider your child as an individual*

> 'A child should not be permitted to violate the personal rights of others. Parents who do not wish to spoil their children must distinguish between freedom and licence.'
>
> *A.S Neill, Educator*

As adults it is our job to make sure that playing children are safe. They are innocent to the ways of the world. Check the flowers and berries in the garden — they could be poisonous. If you do not know much about plants, ask a health official, or a friend who knows more than you do. Always stay close to playing children, ready to rescue a traumatised child. Explain dangers and advise on what to do: 'This is a spider. You can look, but do not touch *any* spider until you have called me, so I can check to see if it is a dangerous one.'

Do not have medicines lying about even if you have explained the dangers to the child. A small padlock on the bathroom cupboard, and other places where poisons are kept (including cleaning liquids and garden poisons) is a sensible act in homes with small children: placing these items high up is only a tantalising target for the climbing child's endeavours.

WHY ALL THE CAUTION?

Playing children are intensely in the *now*. They sometimes fail to distinguish between game and factual life, having been endowed with a massive amount of imagination, courage, and a little growing body with which they are just starting to get acquainted. (How many of us would be game enough to climb the adult equivalent of a child's slippery dip? You would *need* to imagine that you were Superman!)

Children are also insatiably curious, have a drive to explore and make sense of their world, and need this overdose of courage in order to keep trying to learn what they need to know. This is why so many accidents occur — many of them fatal — in early childhood.

Our role is not to hold children back — forbidden fruit is extra sweet — but to try to be totally conscious of the children's whereabouts and activities, and to encourage and challenge them while accepting fully our roles as guides, protectors, caretakers, and nurturers.

DOES MY CHILD HAVE A LEARNING DIFFICULTY?

Probably not. Most parents worry needlessly because they do not see enough children to gain a clear insight into just how individually each child develops. But some children *do* have a learning difficulty, and these are sometimes hard to spot. Learning difficulties often appear as a combination of real clumsiness, lack of attention span, speech problems, and colour confusion.

COLOUR READINESS

If a four-year-old child is having trouble remembering the names of the primary colours (red, blue and yellow) it could be your first warning sign of a later reading difficulty, especially if the child also has other difficulties as mentioned above. Colours are among the first symbols children recognise. If a child has a problem in distinguishing the names of these, then letters, words, lines and numerals may prove equally difficult.

If your four-year-old confuses colour names, test him for colour-blindness by asking him to sort some red, blue and yellow objects into three distinct categories. Try some other colours. If he does this correctly, he is not colour-blind, and the nature of his problem is more likely to be symbolic.

REMEDIAL ACTION

Try the following method to reinforce colour recognition:

Teach the child one colour at a time, starting with red.

Do not ask the child what the colour is. Hold up the ball saying: 'This is red.'

Then ask: 'What is it?'

The child should then respond: 'It is red.' Or simply 'Red.'

Upon the correct response, say: 'That's right, good boy! The ball is red,' repeating and reinforcing the colour-name.

Point out red objects throughout the day when appropriate. Continue this method until the child names a red object correctly on his own accord. Then move on to the colour blue and follow the method above. Continue through the colours. Should the child confuse colours again, go back to teaching the colour he confused until he is able to name the colour correctly again.

During this time present the colour puzzle (p. 58), and play colour-hunt: 'Can you find and bring me three red things?'

THE CHILD WITH SPECIAL NEEDS

Children with special needs must have more repetition than others. All the activities in this book are well suited to such a child and can be repeated over and over again until a skill is learnt.

SHAPING

Children can benefit from practice and learn movements by being 'shaped' into the correct physical activity. Actions to shape may include: clapping; waving; tapping and stroking. To follow is a suggested method of shaping.

1 *Firmly guide child's fingers, hands, or other body parts into required movement*
2 *Praise child enthusiastically*
3 *Repeat until child's voluntary movements seem to correspond with yours*
4 *Encourage child to try on her own*
5 *Praise*
6 *Repeat 1 and 2 until child can carry out the task unaided with reasonable competence*

Shape the child's hands by guiding them into required movements.

The child's hands are being shaped into a clapping action.

Repeat the actions several times, then let the child try unaided.

PREPARATION

As a child learns by observation and imitation, it is a good idea to let him watch you prepare the activities and make the learning materials, rather than wait until he has gone to bed.

Children *do* admire their parents and want to emulate them. They need to see them doing what they do best, to experience their parents as workers, and as committed members of society. In today's world, the time a child spends with his parents is limited. But it is possible to invite him to your workplace as a special treat, and to let him go along to an occasional meeting at night. Seeing you in these situations, as well as watching you prepare his activities, is part of the child's education.

ACTIVITIES – RECOMMENDED AGES

On page 108 each activity for children has been listed under a recommended age — this is a suggested age, a child who is older could certainly benefit and gain pleasure from the same activity.

MESS

Some of the activities in this book are bound to be messy. With such activities the use of an apron, an adult's old thick shirt, or similar protective clothing along with play-clothes that do not matter much will give the child confidence to experiment, and leave you happy about the mess. Mess *is* an aspect of children's creativity and should not be discouraged — hands can be washed, floors and tables wiped. The kitchen is a good place for carrying out the activities and a good 'mess limit' is to have the child work at the table only, thereby protecting the rest of the house.

'Most of the games children play are not invented by themselves . . . the games are a form of lore, a tradition which . . . reaches back into tribal origin.'

George Dennison, Author of 'Lives of Children'

LENGTH OF ACTIVITY TIME

Mornings are recommended for activity time as the child is then most alert, but the tasks can be enjoyed equally well at other times of the day.

Spending 10 or 15 minutes at a choice of one or two activities may make the difference between a long drawn-out day with a child bent on creating misdeeds in search of attention, and an inspired child who is easy to get along with because he got total attention for a short time at the start of the day. A golden rule is: *always pack away before the child tires of the game.* That way he will want to come back for more the next time.

By age four to five years, the child will spend more of his own time with these activities. But during the first 10 or 15 minutes, your presence and attention is needed in order to make the time enjoyable, meaningful and safe. Your child will then feel connected with you, and will demand less of your time for the rest of the day.

Right: Find a place in the house — if there is room the kitchen is ideal — where you can display your child's work. In having the child's creative art prominently shown on a pinboard or refrigerator you are giving value and importance to the child and his work.

14

Most parents feel a degree of guilt at some time. The guilty parent, in fact, is often born simultaneously with the child.

We could always do more for our child. We could give more time, be more understanding, be more generous, say 'no' less often, and so on. A child senses the guilt and uses it to her own advantage. And why not, after all, we did, too!

So how much is enough? The expression 'quality time' has been around for quite a while now, and has been used increasingly as more mothers have returned to work. Quality time means that the time spent with the child is intimate and enjoyable, regardless of how long it is. Spending a quarter of an hour with your child doing one of the many activities in this book is the type of quality referred to — as well as lots of cuddles and 'I love you's.

In order for you to be a well-functioning adult you, too, need space and time off. When you feel that you need to be quiet, or do something alone, or that you have answered enough questions, explain this simply to the child. Children are very direct themselves, and appreciate honesty.

So, if you *have* spent quality time with your child and she keeps pestering for more than you are prepared to give, say *no* and do not feel guilty.

Reading

You will notice that the activities presented in the 3Rs section are not always to the point. For instance, what has making a necklace to do with reading? Educators have found many sub-structures in reading skill, writing skill, and mathematics. The activities presented here all lead towards and will add up to, an accumulated knowledge of the above skills. And — surprisingly — rather than a lot of hard work, they are actually great fun! There is a widely held belief that learning to read is a mysterious process which requires expert teaching skills and is extremely difficult. But this is just a myth. The truth is that if you teach it gradually as outlined here, it becomes part of daily life, another skill which the child will naturally want to master.

SIGNS OF BEGINNING
READING

Just as a baby babbles during the process of learning to speak, a young child pretends to read. Other signs are that he turns pages, spends time alone looking at books, asks for books to be read, asks what street signs mean and recognises letters and words.

Here are some of the concepts that a child who's learning to read will need to know: *first, last, before, after, capital, lower case, word, letter, line, left/right-hand, same, different, sounds of letters and the alphabet.* You

'Regardless of method or motivation, most of those who try to teach pre-schoolers to read in any consistent way are generally successful.'

Joan Beck,
Author

will find games which deal with these concepts throughout this section.

READING STORIES

Reading experts claim that the 'L-A-P' method is the only sure way of teaching a child to read. They literally mean what they say, and recommend a daily or at least a near-daily time spent with your child on your lap, or in some other affectionate position, reading a picture book or two or telling a longer fairytale. Reading experts apart, there is nothing more cosy than reading your child a good-night story. It tends to smooth over unpleasant incidents and possible hurt feelings which are often part of a day, re-establishing your relationship at the end of the day.

Early childhood educators frown upon certain children's publications and tend to favour stories written by distinguished children's authors. Children, however, do not always agree with those choices and get fads on popular books that occasionally flood the market. Gone seem to be the days when schoolteachers forbade the reading of comics and proclaimed that reading comics was not reading. Now educators are using specially designed comic reading primers, having realised that the only way to interest the child is through the child's own interest.

As with everything else, a bit of both 'good' and 'not-so-good' children's literature is probably the most sensible approach.

Most libraries have a very good selection of children's books, or can obtain the book you may be seeking from other libraries. Most urban libraries also offer a story-telling time with the children's librarian reading. The reading is often followed up with a related craft activity, and is worth a regular visit.

When telling a story try to make it as lively as possible. There are books available on how to best present children's literature, should you need to expand your own knowledge in this area. You can also keep up with the latest prize-winning titles through the weekend newspaper reviews.

If you are an avid reader yourself you know how books which deal with your current interests keep your attention. The same applies to a child. Try to find stories which relate to the child's innermost feelings and interests. If she is frightened of the dark, for instance, read *Bedtime for Frances* by Russell Hoban, Harper and Row, NY, 1960. If you are looking for a particular theme, a bookshop assistant or your children's librarian will know how to locate an appropriate book. If you and your child find a particular story delightful, seek out other books by the same author. Chances are that you will enjoy these as well.

You can occasionally dramatise a story by playfully being the Big Bad Wolf, for instance, while your child takes the roles of the three pigs in turn.

Another good dramatic activity is to involve your child and a young visitor in a game of 'mime and guess'. One child can act out something which the other child has to guess. Do not forget to have a turn first: children learn by observation, too.

Read some books yourself before reading them to your child and examine the values they convey. You may not agree with some values, such as sexist language or illustrations, unrealistic or incorrect language, or illustrations which are out of proportion or culturally inappropriate. Reading a child's book critically in this way enables you to make up your own mind as to the type of literature you would like your child exposed to. The choice is yours: you do not have to read a book merely because it is available.

Following is a list of some children's books which are worth getting acquainted with. This list is by no means comprehensive, but may guide you to select publications of similar quality.

Appropriate age: 1 year

GROWING, Fiona Pragoff, Victor Gollancz, 1989
SPOT'S TOY BOX, illustrated by Eric Hill, Heinemann, 1991
THE BABY'S CATALOGUE, Janet and Allan Ahlberg, hardcover: Viking Kestrel, 1982, paperback: Picture Puffin
FIRST THINGS FIRST: A BABY'S COMPANION, Charlotte Voake, Walker, 1988
RIDE A COCK HORSE, selected by Sarah Williams, illustrated by Ian Beck, Oxford, 1986

Appropriate age: 2 years

WATCH ME, illustrated by Pamela Allen, Nelson, 1985
EACH PEACH PEAR PLUM Janet and Allen Ahlberg, hardcover: Viking Kestrel, 1978, paperback: Picture Puffin
ONE WOOLLY WOMBAT, Rod Trinca and Kerry Argent, hardcover: Omnibus, 1982, paperback: Picture Puffin

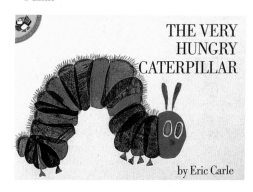

THE VERY HUNGRY CATERPILLAR, Eric Carle, hardcover: Hamish Hamilton, 1970, paperback: Picture Puffin

GO DUCKS GO, Maurice Burns, illustrated by Ron Brooks, hardcover: Deutsch, paperback: Ashton Scholastic, 1987
WE'RE GOING ON A BEAR HUNT, written by Michael Rosen, illustrated by Helen Oxenbury, Walker, 1989
THE MOTHER GOOSE TREASURY, Raymond Briggs, hardcover: Hamish Hamilton, 1966, paperback: Picture Puffin

Appropriate age: 3 years

WHERE THE WILD THINGS ARE, Maurice Sendak, hardcover: Bodley Head, 1962, paperback: Picture Puffin
ALL IN ONE PIECE, Jill Murphy, Walker, 1989
MR GUMPY'S OUTING, John Burningham, hardcover: Cape, 1970, paperback: Picture Puffin
THE SHOPPING BASKET, John Burningham, Cape, 1980
THERE'S A HIPPOPOTAMUS ON OUR ROOF EATING CAKE, written by Hazel Edwards, Illustrated by Deborah Niland, Hodder and Stoughton, 1980

THERE'S A SEA IN MY BEDROOM, written by Margaret Wild, illustrated by Jan Tanner, hardcover: Nelson, 1984, paperback: Picture Puffin
GORILLA, Anthony Browne, Julia MacRae, 1983
SUNSHINE, Jan Ormerod, hardcover: Viking Kestrel, 1981, paperback: Picture Puffin
WINDOW, Jeannie Baker, Random Century Group, 1991
ABC, written and illustrated by Dr. Seuss, Collins, 1964

Appropriate age: 4 years

THE BOY WITH TWO SHADOWS, written by Margaret Mahy, illustrated by Jenny Williams, Dent, 1987
ONE SUNDAY, written by Libby Gleeson, illustrated by John Winch, hardcover and paperback: Angus & Robertson, 1988
CRUSHER IS COMING, Bob Graham, Lothian, 1987
MURGATROYD'S GARDEN, written by Judy Zavos, illustrated by Drahos Zak, hardcover: Heinemann, 1986, paperback: Mandarin

DRAC AND THE GREMLIN, written by Allan Baillie, illustrated by Jane Tanner, hardcover: Viking Kestrel, 1988, paperback: Picture Puffin

Appropriate age: 5 years

'PARDON?' SAID THE GIRAFFE, Colin West, Walker, 1986
THE SMELLY BOOK, Babette Cole, Cape, 1987
THE BUNYIP OF BERKELEY'S CREEK, written by Jenny Wagner, illustrated by Ron Brooks, Picture Puffin, 1973
THE CAR RIDE, John Burningham, Walker, 1984
FRED, Posy Simmonds, hardcover: Cape, 1987, paperback: Picture Puffin
OSCAR GOT THE BLAME, Tony Ross, Anderson/Century Hutchinson 1987
THE CAT IN THE HAT, Dr Seuss, Collins, 1957
FUNNYBONES, written and illustrated by Janet and Allan Ahlberg, hardcover: Heinemann, 1980, paperback, Picture Lions

The following create pre—reading/ reading opportunities for children.

BABY'S OWN BOOK

Materials

thick artist's cardboard (from art
   supply shop)
clear self-adhesive plastic
round curtain rings, 3 cm diameter
thick red or black felt pen
pictures from magazines (or your
   own collage/drawings)
baby's own photo
metal skewer or 2-hole punch
scissors
glue

Method

Cut out 20 x 15 cm pieces of cardboard for pages.

Choose pictures from magazines which most resemble child's favourite toys, activities, foods (toast, cup, dog, and so on), preferably objects your child can already name, or tries to. Cut out neatly.

Glue one or perhaps a few of the pictures onto both sides of each cardboard, leaving a 5 cm margin on the side. Write the name of the object in correct cursive script (see p. 109) under each picture. Cover with clear self-adhesive plastic. Use baby's photo on the front cover and write, 'This is (child's name)'s book.'

Skewer or punch two holes into cardboard pages (make sure holes are in the same spot on each page). Assemble all pages with curtain rings — they allow the child to turn the pages right around like babies do without breaking the back of the book. Read this book often for the child.

Follow Up

Using ordinary white cardboard and the felt pen, write the words you used in the book with large letters on small cards (i.e. 10 x 10 cm or however long the word requires the card to be). The length of the word is unimpor-tant — longer words are not harder to learn to sight—read than shorter words. Do not forget to include a card with the child's own name.

Method

Tell the child five of the words, his most favourite items, including his name. Tell the child like this: 'Look . . . this word says . . .' 'And this word says . . .' and so on through the five words. Do this for the next few days once or twice a day. It should only take a few minutes.

time to introduce five more words from his book of favourite things. Continue this method, adding more words to his word-game until he knows all the words in the book. Remember to ask him to name his old words before the new ones. This reinforces his confidence, as well as reminding him of the words.

Finally, when he knows all the words on the cards, ask him to match them in the book: 'Can you find this word on this page?' When the child can successfully do this, ask him to read one page at a time. This activity can be carried out equally well with any pre-school–aged child.

Next, spread the cards out in front of him and ask him to point to his name. If he points correctly, praise him enthusiastically. If he points to the wrong card, show him the correct one, and go on naming the rest of the five cards. When your child can point correctly to all the five cards, it is time to ask him what each card says. When you are confident that he genuinely knows all the words, it is

Below: Familiar objects from a child's environment can be used in the book as they are easy for him to recognise and name.

ICING

Materials
1 cup icing sugar
2 tablespoons powdered cocoa
2 tablespoons boiling water
hundreds and thousands
child's brush

Method

Child sifts icing sugar and cocoa into clean saucepan.

You gradually add boiling water and stir over heat until warm and smooth.

Child paints onto cool biscuits and sprinkles with hundreds and thousands.

ALPHABET BISCUITS

A fun way for children to familiarise themselves with letter shapes.

Materials
1 cup self raising flour
1/2 tablespoon cornflour
1/3 cup butter
1 egg
1/4 cup sugar

Method

Ask child to help with following:

Sift flour, cornflour into a bowl.

Rub in butter.

Add beaten egg and sugar.

Knead into dough, turn onto floured table and roll small pieces into sausages.

Write out letters about 8 cm tall and 4 cm wide on greaseproof paper and have child shape dough sausages onto the letters — try spelling out child's own name.

Flatten, and slide onto greased tray.

Bake in moderate oven (180°C) for about 25 minutes.

Cool on cake rack.

RHYMING GAMES

Select various nursery rhymes which are your child's favourite, and which she knows by heart. Then start reciting, leaving out the last rhyming word, as follows:

Little Jack Horner
Sat in a . . .
and wait for the child to fill in the missing word.

NURSERY RHYMES

Little Jack Horner

Sat in a corner

Eating a Christmas pie

He put in his thumb

And pulled out a plum

And said 'What a good boy am I.'

Humpty Dumpty sat on a wall

Humpty Dumpty had a great fall

All the King's horses and all the King's men

Couldn't put Humpty together again.

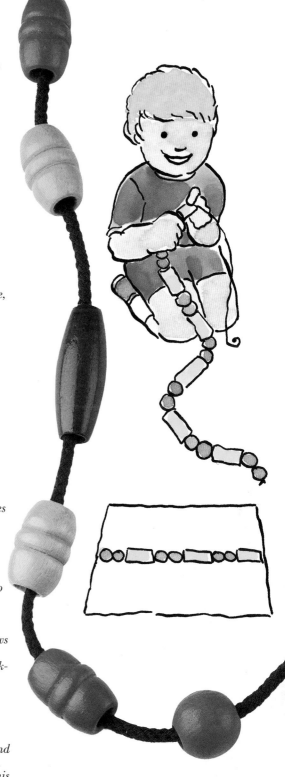

Jack and Jill went up the hill

To fetch a pail of water.

Jack fell down and broke his crown

And Jill came tumbling after.

Twinkle twinkle little star

How I wonder what you are.

Up above the world so high

Like a diamond in the sky.

Twinkle twinkle little star

How I wonder what you are.

Mary Mary quite contrary

How does your garden grow?

With silver bells and cockle shells,

And pretty maids all in a row.

Molly my sister and I fell out

And what do you think it was all

about?

She loved coffee and I loved tea,

And that was the reason we couldn't

agree.

NECKLACE THREADING

Following a selected pattern involves reading and recognising an image.

Materials

beads in a variety of shapes and colours (preferably wooden, from craft and wool shops)

white cardboard cards, 10 x 20 cm

felt pens, matching in colour to beads

threading lace, or long shoelace

clear self-adhesive plastic (optional)

Method

Draw beads in patterns of your choice, different patterns on each card. For instance, two round red beads followed by two square green beads, then two round red beads again.

Cover with plastic for longer life.

The Game

Child chooses a card and follows pattern, making a necklace. Continues the same pattern until necklace is complete. You can point out to child to follow (or read) pattern from left to right.

Child removes beads and follows another card, or let him wear the necklace.

Variation

Allow child to explore shapes and colours of beads and to make up his own pattern, not necessarily in any sequential order. Also see p.72 Dyed macaroni.

ALPHABET SOUP AND T-SOUP

Search for, and recognition of capital letter shapes.

Materials
alphabet noodles
soup stock

Method

Cook enough stock to make a cupful of soup and add alphabet noodles. Simmer until letters are cooked. Have for lunch.

T-Soup Variation

Pour into a bowl a tablespoon of alphabet noodles.

Quickly remove the numerals, and offer the bowl of uncooked noodles to the child.

Ask child to find all the Ts (or other letter) that are hiding amongst the letters.

Cook only the Ts in the soup.

Other Variations

Ask child to find all the letters in his first name and/or his surname.

Write out all the printed capitals, so he can locate and match the letters.

Ask the child to sort all the alphabet letters into separate ice-cube trays (26 cubes are needed).

NB! Do not be surprised if child starts playing 'cooking' with the noodles. If this occurs, let him play. Then later, return to the sorting game.

HINTS ON INTRODUCING NEW WORDS

Introduce the word thoroughly and slowly, e.g.: 'You see this word TO? The t's hat has slid down its tummy.' Make the letters come alive like this so the child notices and remembers the word. Demonstrate the word in a sentence like this: 'This word says TO, like: I want TO eat icecream (emphasise word).'

Then take the next word and think of something special to say about the way it looks. Go through all the words in this way. Then follow guidelines on how to teach words in Baby's Own Book *on page 20.*

TAPING STORIES

Instruments can be used to define the end of the page.

Materials

a favourite storybook
cassette recorder
cassette
musical instrument

Method

Suggest to child that you record one of his favourite stories. Let him choose one himself.

Find a musical instrument, such as a bell, to use when turning the pages of the story.

Let the child take the parts he remembers by heart. Or you can be the storyteller, and he can be all the characters by changing his voice, sounding squeaky or gruff. He could also sound the instrument when you turn each page. Record the story.

Listen to the recording, and have a good giggle together!

TELEVISION VIEWING

Shows which feature violence can be detrimental to the child's personality development, social development and view of the world. Keep in mind that children tend to confuse fantasy with reality and that they learn from observation. Television programs should be chosen with the same care as the books you read for him.

MOST IMPORTANT WORDS

Familiarisation of the written image of frequently used words.

Materials

flash-card sized cardboard (14 x 7 cm)
thick red or black felt pen

Method

Ask child to name friends, pets, etc. Write 'Mum', 'Dad', sister's and brother's names, favourite colour, game, toy. Include feeling words that the child knows and uses, such as love, hugs, kiss, hate, scarey.

ALPHABET BINGO

Matching letter shapes – upper- and lower-case.

Materials

white cardboard or paper
thick black felt pen
ruler
scissors

Method

Cut out four 28 x 16 cm rectangles from the white board.

Divide two boards into two lengthwise with a ruled line and breadthwise into 7 equal spaces so that you have 14 spaces in total. Repeat on the other side.

Using the correct upper- and lower-case cursive letters (see p. 109) write one of each upper-case letter onto the two boards so that one board covers A-M and the other N-Z, each with one blank space left over. Write all the corresponding lower-case letters on the other side of the pre-ruled boards. These will remain the boards in the Bingo game.

Next, rule up one side of the two remaining boards, and write upper-case letters A-M and N-Z on one side as before. Cut the boards up along the

black lines, so that you are left with two whole boards, and with 26 cards with upper-case letters, and two blank cards (you do not need these).

ALPHABET PUZZLE

Child can use letters as a puzzle, matching the capital letters on the cards to the boards.

BINGO SKILL GAME

Spread out A,B,C,D, and E cards on the floor in front of the child. Teach the child all the upper-case letter names of the alphabet as follows: 'This is the letter A. What is it?' 'This is the letter B. What is it?' And so on until E. Repeat.

Now ask child to point to letter A, etc.

When child points to correct letter, acknowledge him enthusiastically. If child points to the incorrect letter, simply move his finger to point to the correct letter, saying: '*This* is B, that's right.'

Play this game for five minutes each day until child knows upper- and lower-case letters.

A B C D E F G
H I J K L M
N O P Q R S T
U V W X Y Z

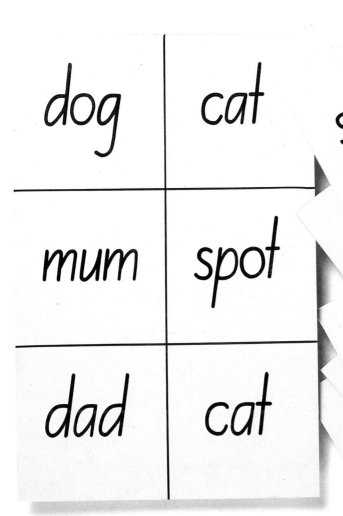

again in the spot they were previously.

The skill is to remember where the

letters are.

Play, taking turns, until all letters

have been matched.

Variation

An easier version is to use only upper-

case OR lower-case cards. Have two

each of upper-case cards or lower-case

cards, and play as above.

WORD BINGO

Materials
cardboard
thick felt pen

Method

Cut out two boards 30 x 20 cm and

divide into 6 rectangles each.

Write out 6 of your child's new words

on both.

Cut one board up into 6 cards.

The Game

Child picks a card and matches on his

board.

When all six words are found he

announces Bingo. (This is just

matching each word, or a puzzle.)

When child can match 12 words, you

can make two boards with 12 cards,

and both play, having one board

each.

BINGO

Hold up a letter and child has to call
out if it is on his board. If it is, give
him the card.

When his board is filled up with
matching cards, he calls out *Bingo*.

Mix cards and let him hold up the
cards (you both play, using one board
each).

Variations

Draw up two more boards with lower-

case letters on them, and cut into

cards.

Now you can play Bingo with the

boards turned up with capital letters,

but using lower-case cards, or vice-

versa.

Play MEMORY, using upper- and

lower-case cards, A-M and a-m.

How to play Memory: Help each other

face all cards down so that blank side

faces up. Mix them around well, and

separate, so that they do not overlap.

Each player takes a turn at turning

two cards face up. If they match (A

and a), the player keeps them and has

another turn. If they do not match,

the player turns them upside down

LISTENING SKILLS GAME—MATCH THE SOUNDS

Listening skills are vital for recognition of sounds/letters in words.

M a t e r i a l s

8 matchboxes,
margarine containers with lids, or toilet rolls stapled securely at both ends
colourful adhesive plastic cover
grains of rice
shell noodles
dry beans
almonds
Sellotape

M e t h o d

Place a couple of sprinkles of rice in two boxes, and repeat with the noodles, beans and almonds so that there are two containers of each sort. Close and Sellotape or staple openings for safety. Cover all eight containers with the same cover, so that they look identical when covered.

T h e G a m e

Ask child to pick a container and shake. Ask child to find another box that sounds just the same. Do not help child.

If child is mistaken, shake them both, one at a time, saying to the child, 'Listen carefully! Does this sound (shake one box) sound like this sound (shake other box)?' If child still says 'yes', ask, 'Are you sure? Let us listen to them all . . .', shaking one at a time until you find the correct one. 'Now listen — can you hear that these two sound the same? Now let us try to match another two.'

V a r i a t i o n

Play Memory with sound boxes (see p. 27) by shaking only two for each turn.

SOUND HUNT

A challenging game to find objects that begin with a certain letter sound.

M a t e r i a l s
cardboard
thick felt pen
blackboard

M e t h o d

When your child asks you what you can do today, tell her that you are going to play a sound-hunting game. 'I thought we would hunt around for things which have the sound terh in it, like toothbrush. See if you can find some things for me that have terh in them, while I close my eyes and wait here.'

Child is to find objects with the sound of T in them. If she has difficulty whisper a few items in her ear (teddy, top etc.)

Place found things in a pile.

At the end of the game ask child to hand you all the terh objects one by one and write down what they are on pieces of cardboard or on her blackboard.

Ask her to draw pictures of the objects on the back of the cards or on the blackboard to match each word.

MATCH SOUNDS TO CASSETTE RECORDER

Developing the skills of listening and concentration.

Materials

cassette recorder
cassette
about six items that make sounds, such as an egg-beater, child's musical instrument, scissors and paper, chunky necklaces etc.

Method

When your child is not around, record the sounds of the items clearly.

The Game

Place recorded items spaced out on the floor and tell the child that you have a new game: he is to listen carefully to the recording, and find the item he thinks made the sound. Play the first sound.

If child selects the wrong item, replay cassette and ask him to listen to the recorded sound again.

Ask child to make sound with selected item. 'Is it the same sound as on the tape recorder, or is it different?' . . . 'OK, try again . . .'

Variation

Record the following: toilet flushing; phone ringing; doorbell ringing (if you have one); cat meowing (no hints on how you can arrange this); vacuum cleaner going; tap running; car engine; and other sounds which are familiar to your child.

Ask child to guess each sound.

A good hint is to write down each recorded sound as you are recording, because it is quite amazing how easy it is to forget the source.

TELL ME A STORY

While story telling the child is practicing building a sentence and developing the structure.

Materials

cassette recorder

Method

Ask child to tell you a story: 'I always tell you stories — today it is your turn. Can you tell me a story?' Remember that a story has a beginning, a middle and an end. Guide the child accordingly. '. . . and what happened at the end?' Record.

If child gets stuck, ask leading questions with wide eyes, like: '. . . and what happened then?'

Listen to the story on the cassette recorder.

Variation

Make up a story together. You start the story, then pause. Child continues. You take up the story-line anew, until story seems to be finished.

Listen to recording.

(Make the story personal so that the child can relate to it, using her name; 'Once I knew a little girl named . . . and her cat's name was . . .' Prompt 'your turn' if necessary.)

Write upper-case letters on one cube; lower-case on other.

DICE GAME

Recognising upper- and lower-case letters.

Materials

2 empty milk cartons
felt pen
four strips 7 x 21 cm paper
glue
white masking tape
clear self-adhesive plastic

Method

Cut three of the carton's four sides down to 7 x 7 cm, cutting the fourth side so that it can be bent to be a lid which fits inside. Use masking tape to tape down firmly.

Cut two strips of 7 x 21 cm paper. Divide strips by folding into 3 equal (7 cm) squares. Unfold, and glue onto cube, so that all squares are now covered.

Write out A-F on one cube with upper-case letters, and a-f with lower-case letters on the other cube (see p. 109) for correct script.

Cover with clear self-adhesive plastic (optional).

The Game

Take turns rolling dice until they match, rolling one at a time.

Clap when die match (for instance, E + e).

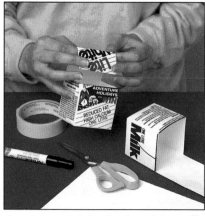

Cut down 3 of the 4 sides of the milk carton. Bend in lid.

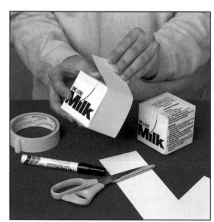

Coat on glue and cover squares with white paper.

MAKE-A-BOOK

Expanding Baby's Own Book on p.20, developing new concepts.

Materials

small exercise book (blank)
camera
film with 12 pictures
glue
felt pen

Method

Show child how to take a photo. Child takes 12 photos of his choice.

Have photos developed the same day.

Glue photos into exercise book, and write child's dictated captions beneath each photo (see p. 109 for writing correct script, or use typewriter).

Read this book whenever child requests it.

LABELLING

A great way to connect the written word with the actual object.

Materials

10 x 10 cm or 10 x ? cm cardboard cards (size depends on length of word)
thick felt pen
masking tape

Method

Write out names of objects in the house in correct script (p. 109), and fasten onto objects (for instance, bed, fridge, TV, chair).

If child asks you what you are writing, tell him 'I am writing the word chair. *Would you like to help me by sticking it on the chair over there?' And the game is on . . .*

MEMORY GAMES

For practicing skills in concentration and observation.

What's Different?

Dress up a doll and ask child to close eyes.* Add or take away from the doll's clothes. For example, add a necklace, take off one shoe, pull sleeve off one arm, change skirt.

Variation

Play the game with one another.

When you are in you could, for example, put on lipstick or take off

one shoe, replace shoes with slippers, or put on a hat or change your blouse.

What's Missing

Lay out five objects. 'Read' them together from left to right; for instance, 'one toy car, one pair of scissors, a button, a block, a vase.'

Repeat 'reading', remembering to read from left to right.

Ask child to close eyes and take away an object without upsetting the order or making a noise.

Say, 'Open your eyes; I bet I can trick you this time. Do you know what's missing?'

See if child remembers what's missing. If not, try to 'read' together in order to jog his memory, pausing when you point to the space left by the missing object.

Variation

When the child is very good at this game, take away two objects, then three objects.

Variation

When the child has become quick at spotting what is missing, start putting out six objects and keep adding objects (up to 10 items) over a period of months.

Variation

Draw a house or person on the blackboard and, while the child has his eyes closed, wipe off a feature or draw an extra item. Try to avoid the squeak of chalk on the blackboard.

* For younger children who do not like to close their eyes (and peek, if they do), you can drape a cloth over the items instead while removing or adding one.

TALKING GAMES

Language is our primary form of communication. Encourage your child to talk freely and to formulate his own ideas. If a child is never listened to (we all know how busy parents comment with 'Mmm. . .' without really listening), he cannot suddenly be expected to express himself. The same applies to school, where children are asked to listen more than to talk; and are then expected to write long sentences.

When language is fluid, reading and writing will come easily. Children often ask us questions. Adults often ask questions of a child only in order to test him, and then correct him with the 'right' information.

THE INTERVIEW

Here is a game which you and your child will both enjoy; there are no right or wrong answers.

Materials
paper
pen
or tape recorder

Method
Without making this activity too staged, gain the child's attention, a good time might be after a short story. Say: I'd like to ask you some questions, and I want to write down (or tape record) your answers. Are you ready?'

The child will probably be a little surprised but continue the interview. Assure the child that you really want to know his answers.

Taping the 'interview' will give you more of an opportunity to listen to the child without being distracted in writing their responses. You'll need to keep the child's thought process and conversation moving, so be quick with your responses.

Some example questions are:

- *Where do you think the sun goes when it gets dark?*
- *Why do the clouds move?*
- *Where is the moon when the sun is shining?*
- *Do you dream and where is your dream?*
- *Where on your body do you think?*
- *What else is this room can think and feel (would perhaps the table)?*

This is a fun game. It is most important to keep the conversation flowing smoothly and not let the child feel that it is a test for right and wrong answers. Do not try to correct the child or offer 'real' answers. The idea is to allow the child to explore a concept through thinking and describing their thoughts, Value the child's thinking process without being judgmental — even if some answers amuse you.

SAMPLE INTERVIEW
Mother with Nicola 4 years 3 months

M: *Do you dream?*

N: *Yes.*

M: *Where are the dreams now?*

N: *In my head.*

M: *Can you see them right now?*

N: *Yes.*

M: *What do you see?*

N: *A leopard dream, a story dream, a fat trick dream.*

M: *And where do the dreams come from?*

N: *From my head.*

M: *Have they always been there?*

N: *Yes.*

M: *Even when you were in your mummy's tummy?*

N: *No — they were in my tummy.*

M: *How did they get in there?*

N: *Through my head into my tummy, it starts from here (she points to the middle of her forehead).*

M: *Where do my dreams come from?*

N: *From your head.*

M: *Who puts them in there?*

N: *God.*

READING MACHINE

The child can progressively learn to sound out new words using the reading machine.

Materials

3 empty 1 litre milk cartons
3 paper strips (7 x 29.5 cm)
thick felt pen
paper towel rack with removable rod, or other rod-type rack
clear self-adhesive plastic (optional)
glue

will have to choose amongst these consonants — and choose 4 vowels (a,e,i,o,u) on the third cube, writing one letter on each square.

Cover with clear adhesive plastic (optional).

Pierce sides of cubes exactly at centre and make holes to fit onto rod. Smooth holes, making it easier for cubes to turn.

Fit cubes on rod so that the cube with the vowels is in the centre.

letters face her, and sounds out word. She will need your help in the beginning.

Method

Make milk cartons into cubes (see p. 30 for instructions).

Glue one paper strip around each cube, leaving two end pieces bare.

Using correct script (p. 109) write 8 consonants (b,c,d,f,g,h,j,l,m,n,p,r,s, t,w,z,y) on two of the cubes — you

Your child now has a reading machine.

Variation

For a more permanent reading machine, use wooden blocks instead of milk cartons.

The Game

Child turns cubes so that all three

CLOUD SHAPES

For language development encourage your child to describe their imaginative thoughts freely.

Method

Lie spread-eagled on a grassy space.

Shade eyes and look for faces and other shapes in the clouds. Allow the imagination to lead the game.

WHAT'S THAT SIGN?

Use signs that the child may've noticed on the street for a concentration and recognition game.

Materials

2 copies of the *Highway Code* (from HMSO)
2 each of same magazine with pictures of shop signs/other
1 sheet of cardboard
glue
clear self-adhesive plastic

Method

Cut out most appropriate signs, i.e. stop sign, children crossing sign, school sign, give way sign, and so on from both traffic handbooks, and/or similarly clear shop signs (2 of each) from magazines or other sources.

Glue these onto approximately 8 x 6 cm cards cut out from cardboard.

Allow to dry.

Cover with plastic for longer wear.

The Game

Play Memory game (see p. 27) with your child. Unless the child asks, it is not necessary to tell the child what the signs mean initially, as this will naturally be mentioned during the game sooner or later. ('Where do you think the other stop sign might be, Nick, can you remember?')

Children going to school

No cycling

Roundabout

Stop and give way

Quayside or river bank

No pedestrians

Accompanied horses

Loose chippings

A	B	C	D	E	F
a	be	call	did	eat	fall
about	because	came	do	eight	far
after	been	can	does	every	fast
again	before	carry	done		find
all	best	clean	don't		first
am	better	cold	down		five
and	big	come	drink		fly
any	black	could			four
are	blue	cut			found
around	both	cry			for
as	bring				from
ask	brown				full
at	but				funny
ate	buy				
away	by				

SENTENCE MAKER

Build and practice reading a small sentence from familiar words.

Method

When your child knows all the words in his book (see p. 20), add on more of his favourite words. As he becomes more accustomed to the magic of words, you can say to him, 'Ask me for any word that you want', adding one word each day to his sight-vocabulary (words he recognizes by heart).

Soon you and he will be able to construct whole sentences by spreading out the cards and combining the words. You may find that those small 'glue' words are missing, so here is a list of such words. They are also some of the most commonly recurring words in print.

A suggested way to use a sentence maker is to ask the child a question; which they verbally answer then they can try to find the words to make up the answer from the board.

K	L	M	N	O	P
keep	laugh	made	never	of	pick
kind	let	make	new	old	play
know	like	many	no	on	please
kiss	little	me	not	once	pretty
	live	much	now	one	pull
	long	my		only	put
	love	myself		open	
	look			or	
				our	
				out	
				over	

U	V	W			Y
under	very	walk	we	who	yellow
up		want	well	why	yes
us		warm	went	will	you
use		was	were	wish	your
		wash	what	with	
			when	work	
			where	write	
			which		
			white		

G	H	I
gave	had	I
get	has	if
give	have	in
go	he	into
goes	help	is
going	her	it
good	here	its
got	him	it's
green	his	
grow	hold	
	hot	
	how	
	hurt	

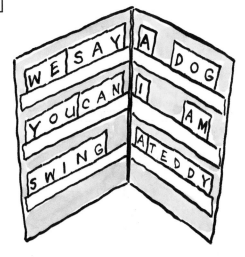

R	S	T
ran	said	take
read	sat	tell
red	saw	ten
ride	say	thank
right	see	that
round	seven	then
run	she	them
	show	the
	sing	there
	sit	these
	six	they
	sleep	this
	small	those
	so	three
	some	to
	soon	too
	start	two
	stop	

MOVEMENT CARDS

Physical actions can assist in the process of word recognition from flash cards.

Materials
flash-card-sized cardboard
(10 x ? cm)
thick felt pen

Method

Write out movement words: jump, run, skip, hop, gallop, walk and so on.

The Game

Teach new words as on p. 24.

Flash card, and ask child to demonstrate what the card says by jumping, etc.

WORD SCRAMBLE

Creating words from letters can be a fun way of learning to sound out words.

Materials
lower-case letters in correct script (see p. 109). Write:
b,c,d,f,g,h,l,m,n,p,r,s,t and
a,e,i,o,u.

Method

Turn letters upside down and ask child to pick three while you also pick three. Turn cards over so that letters face up.

Child tries to make a word with his cards, while you also try to make a word with yours.

If one of the players has either all vowels, or all consonants, reshuffle.

It is correct to make a word with one or two letters only (such as 'a' or 'it').

Variation

Make two or more words with the letters dealt to each player.

Add more letters as skills increase.

Follow Up

Buy a Scrabble game.

Writing

ABC books and street signs expose children to printed upper-case letters. Parents also tend to teach children to write their name with these letters because straight lines appear to be easier. School-teachers are resentful of parents who do this, especially when the letter shape has been taught incorrectly.

It is better to start teaching both upper- and lower-case letters from the beginning (see page 109). This will prevent the child from having to unlearn and start again, as well as being presented with the conflict of whether to believe you or the teacher.

Use capitals only at the start of names, and where words follow a full stop, with lower-case letters for the remainder of the name, word, and sentence. When writing, say, a caption to the child's drawing, try to remember to commence writing on the left-hand side of the page so that the child's eye becomes used to looking for the printed word where reading on the page normally begins.

It is best to teach a child the terms 'lower-case' and 'upper-case' rather than 'little a' and 'big A'. Children's minds are extremely logical and cannot make sense of *big* and *little*, because the letters do not always look big or little, especially if a child starts to write them.

MIRROR WRITING

All children write some letters and numbers facing the wrong way; for instance, instead of 5 they write Ƨ . Some children even write not just the individual letters back to front, but whole names or words, like this: qᴉoʇ . Do not as a rule point the error out to the child, as she may jump to the conclusion that there is something wrong with her whereas this is merely a normal step in her writing development. Occasionally compare her letter or number with yours and let her tell you if she can see something different. Eventually the tendency will right itself with practice and a growing awareness and attention to detail.

SIGNS OF BEGINNING WRITING

- *painting*
- *drawing*
- *using correct pencil grip (holding pencil between thumb, index and middle fingers)*
- *writing own name*
- *requesting to be shown or told how to write letters and words*

LEFT- OR RIGHT-HANDEDNESS

If you are not sure which hand your child favours, place a crayon on a piece of paper and ask the child to draw a picture. You will immediately note the hand that reaches out for the crayon as his particular preferred handedness. Try the experiment a few times just to be sure, or observe the hand that reaches for other objects throughout the day.

Never teach a left-handed child to cut, draw, or eat with the right hand. It has been found that forcing a left-handed child to become right-handed can result in lack of self esteem, and even linguistic confusion and a stammer in the speech. This may be due to the handedness being connected to left/right brain dominance, and so should not be tampered with.

CONCEPTS

It may be surprising to realise that in order to write, children need to understand concepts such as *under, over, through, line, across, below, above, around, straight, curved, short, tall, long, slanted, top, middle* and *bottom*.

Right: A variety of different surfaces can be used to practice letter shapes.

FEELY BLANKET

Allow children to explore their environment through touch. A Feely Blanket can be used for many ages but for young children — omit buttons and small objects that may be swallowed.

Materials

16 different squares of fabric (25 x 25 cm). The fabrics should be chosen so that they will provide various tactile experiences, for instance, smooth, bumpy, rough, furry, velvety, lumpy, towelling, coolish, scattered pattern lines.

length of plain fabric

contrasting fabric for binding
polyester wadding

sturdy, easy-to-use zip (shorter than one square)

large and small buttons

two large press studs

opening/flap materials (felt)

sturdy shoelaces

velcro

ribbons

other

Method

Make a patchwork quilt of the 16 different fabrics. Turn over, and sew on zip in one square, press studs with an interesting item to press on them on another square, buttons and button holes on another square, and so on, as shown in the diagram.

Leave some squares free; just touching and stroking the various fabrics is an activity in itself for the child. Place wadding in between wrong sides of top layer and bottom layer and pin together. Tack around the edge and trim. Sew buttons at junction of

squares through all thicknesses. Bind around the edge with contrasting fabric.

The Game

Place blanket on the floor or as a wall-hanging. You can show the child some of the interesting extra activities on the surfaces (the zip, ribbons, buttons) so she can get the idea of how to use

---

EYE–HAND COORDINATION AND FINE MOTOR SKILLS

In order to understand the vital concepts, the child needs to be able to carry out tasks which involve her fine motor skills, using the small muscles in her hand, and master the skill of seeing-and-manipulating an object with the hand according to her desire, thought and will. The suggestions and activities in this section all promote the development of these skills.

Method

Designate a sturdy cardboard box for dress-up clothes. Cover with colourful adhesive plastic.

Place in box items of clothing which have zippers, buttons and so on for child to practise on. Dressing up is as popular with boys as with girls, and is an activity well worth offering to the children, not only because it helps them with their dexterity skills, but also because make-believe is the method that children use to try on, comprehend and solidify reality.

them. After that you can leave her to explore at will.

Variation

Make a 'book' with squares instead, using length of two squares, and placing them on top of each other. Stitch in the centre.

DRESSING UP

Valuable for self-expression, language development, social interaction and coordination skills.

Materials

old adult clothes, hats, wigs (well disinfected and washed), uniform caps (police etc, available from disposal stores), shoes, evening clothes, jewellery, bags, capes, and more.

full-length mirror.

WRITING SURFACES AND MEDIUMS

Blackboards are the perfect, always available partner to reading and writing activities. For instance, many of the reading games in this book can comfortably be carried out on a blackboard, rather than on cardboard. There are many ready-made blackboards available in toyshops. Sometimes you can be lucky and pick one up cheaply at a government stores (used school furniture) warehouse.

Blackboards are best if they are big enough for the child to express himself using large arm-movements. If a large blackboard will be too expensive, why not paint a small wall, or the bottom half of the same wall, or a door, with blackboard paint. Give the wall or door two or three coats, and attach a soap holder next to it with dustless chalk, both white and coloured.

Just having a blackboard will encourage the child to draw whenever he walks past it, or on occasions when he feels inspired. You can also encourage drawing by doing some drawings on it yourself (not as a competitor, but just for the enjoyment of it). The blackboard lends itself beautifully to illustrating told stories. Children love it when you somehow involve them: 'Once upon a time . . . (use child's real name) lived in a house (draw child and house) . . .'

Above: Place a blackboard at child's height and encourage him to express himself through drawing. Avoid showing him 'how to draw' objects as seen here.

TYPEWRITERS

If you have an old typewriter, it will prove an exciting way of showing your child how print happens. If you have not got an old manual typewriter, you should be able to find one easily and cheaply because nowadays most people prefer electric typewriters or word processors. You could buy one from an office supplier (explain that it is for your child, and if you're lucky they may even give you one free) or look in the local paper or at garage sales.

It is best to show the child how a typewriter works: how to feed in the paper, how to get to the next line, how to do spacing. You can apply red round stickers on the letters which make up her name, and write the letters with a black felt pen onto the red stickers to highlight them.

- *Type her name.*
- *Ask her what she wants you to type.*
- *Let her dictate you a story (she can illustrate it later).*
- *Let her write on the typewriter however she pleases (remember that the nonsensical practising is the lead-up to the actual skill).*
- *Help her when the letters get stuck together, and explain why it happens (only one letter can be pressed at a time).*

SAND

When you are at the beach one day, show your child how it is possible to write in the sand. Try

Right: It's fun for a child to physically follow sequences they have drawn (see also p.63).

wet sand, and dry sand. If you have a sandpit at home (see p. 90) you could wet some sand and place it on a flat surface, patting it out, drawing and writing on it, and wiping it out when it is no longer wanted.

In Vietnam it is a custom to write out all grievances and sorrows near the surf on the beach, allowing the high tide to wipe it all out and wash it away.

CONCRETE

Remember hopscotch? A box-full of chalk outside on the concrete or asphalt drive will give the children lots of joy. Aside from hopscotch, they can draw and write to their hearts' content.

CHUNKY CRAYONS

It is worthwhile investing in a box of chunky crayons (not the little thin ones) available at good toy shops. They lend themselves so well to being used easily by small fingers and never break (well, almost never).

Chunky crayons and paper should always be available to small children at home. If you worry about walls and furniture, explain the rules about drawing — only on paper with crayons — and take away the crayons for one day if the rule is broken. Remind child about the rule — children learn by repetition.

reels (circle), wooden block (square), wooden triangle, empty matchbox (covered with adhesive plastic or paper) for rectangle.

The Game

Child pushes objects through matching shapes, then opens lid and takes them out in order to start again.

FEELY CARDS

Games involving touch are developing the child's small hand muscles.

Materials

16 cards, 6 x 6 cm
glue
samples of 'feely' materials such as sandpaper, fur, sponge, carpet, bees-wax, leather, velvet, hessian, suede leather, 9 small buttons, 7 headless matchsticks, corrugated cardboard, foil, small ceramic item, shaggy carpet, patterned wallpaper

SHAPE BOX

Eye-hand coordination, shape awareness and problem solving are vital pre-writing skills.

Materials

ice-cream container with lid
stanley knife
objects to fit

Preparation

Cover container with colourful adhesive plastic.

Cut 3 or 4 shapes out of lid, using stanley knife. Suggestions are: circle, square, triangle, rectangle.

Find objects to match: for instance

Method

Cut/arrange materials to fit on cards. Glue on.

The Game

Place cards in pillowcase and ask child to reach arm in and find one. Ask child to describe how it feels (cold, warm, bumpy, furry, rough, smooth).

BOTTLE/JAR-TOP BOX

An activity involving observation and eye-hand coordination.

Materials

large cardboard box
small coffee jar with lid
small plastic drink bottle with lid
jam jar with lid
small tomato sauce bottle with lid
milk bottle with lid
other small jar with screwtop lid
bright paint/colourful self-adhesive plastic

Method

Cover box with self-adhesive plastic, or paint in bright colour.

Place clean jars and lids in box.

The Game

Child opens lids, experiments with fitting them on correct bottle/jar. NB! This activity must be carried out in your presence, as some bottle tops

Below: Recycle household materials to make the Shape Box.

Below: Collect different shaped bottles/jars with tops and store in box for matching activity.

or lids may go in small mouths, and jars can be broken.

Store jars in box and take out on occasions.

FEELY LETTERS

Letter sounds and shapes are practised with these cards.

Materials
cardboard
artist's paintbrush
glue
salt shaker
sand

Method

Cut out cards from cardboard, 10 x 10 cm.

Write out large upper-case letters neatly (see page 109).

Paint over the letter with glue.

Sprinkle liberally with sand (placing sand in fish-and-chip shop type salt shaker works well). Allow to dry.

Shake excess sand off.

The Game

Take child's finger and trace carefully (as if writing) over a letter. Ask child to do the same. Tell child letter name. Repeat with five letters.

Place letters into pillowcase. Ask child to put both hands in and find one card and guess name of letter.

Ask child to pull out letter. If correct, clap enthusiastically, or in some way praise the child. If incorrect, say 'Nearly! It is . . . (give correct letter name).'

SEWING INTO SPONGES

A creative way of developing coordination skills.

Materials
thin (1 cm) sponges (cheap sponge packs are available at supermarkets)
colourful wool
darning or raffia needle

Method

Thread needle with double length of wool and tie ends together into a double knot.

Child sews own pattern into sponge.

Sponge is an easy sewing medium.

FEELY STICKS

Recognising the difference in the texture of materials.

Materials

empty instant cocoa tin
colourful self-adhesive plastic
8 dowel sticks, 24 cm long, 1 cm
 diameter
sandpaper
velvet
fur
bumpy fabric
glue
rubber bands

Method

Cover tin with self-adhesive plastic.

Cut sandpaper, velvet, fur and bumpy fabric so that it fits around dowel stick, and so that only half of stick (12 cm) is covered. Glue on, using two sticks for each type of cover. Wrap rubber bands around glued material until well stuck on.

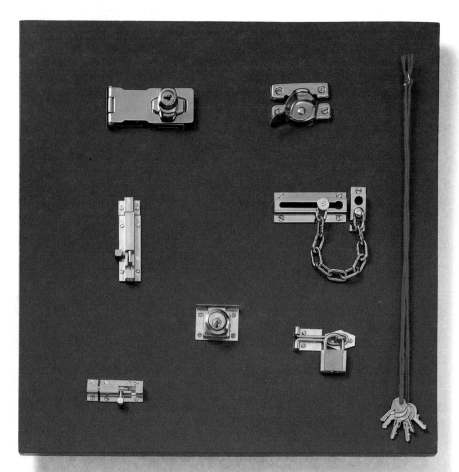

Above: Your local hardware store will have a variety of locks.

The Game

Place feely sticks upside down in tin. Child pulls out one stick and describes how it feels. Then pulls out another stick and describes, adding whether it feels the same or is different from the first stick.

Use blindfold for child over four years of age to make it more difficult.

LOCK BOARD

Some of the locks require fine finger/hand movements to open successfully.

Materials

50 x 50 cm pine board
blue paint
undercoat sealer
locks, all sizes and shapes
 (including padlock)
screws
string

Method

Paint pine board with undercoat sealer and then two coats of paint.

Screw locks on at attractive distance from one another.

Attach keys to a string which will reach all locks, and attach string to the board.

Hang board on the wall as a toy for your child to explore. You can colour-code lock and key with a dot of paint (one pair green, one blue, etc) so that your child can find them more easily.

EYE-DROPPER EXPERIMENT

This is an exercise in fine motor skills and eye–hand coordination. The skill of using an eye-dropper is similar to using pegs and is not easy. You may have to demonstrate a few times.

Materials
- baby food glass jar
- 3 good eye-droppers (one for each colour)
- blotting paper/paper towel
- empty bucket
- jug of water
- red, blue, and yellow dyed water paint

Method

Fill jar with water.

Child fills eye-dropper with selected water colour and drips into jar of clear water. The colour drops will swirl in beautiful patterns in the clean water.

Child selects more colours and repeats procedure. When water in jar is murky, empty into bucket, rinse, and refill with clean water from jug. Start again.

Variation

Child drips colours on paper towel or other absorbent paper.

LEARNING TO LACE

The in out movement of the needlework involves some concentration.

Materials
- pictures from magazines
- cardboard or hessian (15 x 15 cm)
- glue
- skewer
- darning/raffia needle
- colourful wool

Method

Cut out and glue interesting pictures from magazines (cars, houses, children, animals, dolls) onto cardboard.

Skewer holes at 1.5 cm intervals around shape, or, if you are using hessian, draw required shape in the middle of the cloth. The size of the picture should be no larger than 8–10 cm across.

Thread needle with double length of wool and tie together in a double knot.

Child sews on the line on hessian, or through holes in cardboard. Remind the child often to follow the line, or holes.

Be prepared to rescue needle from many tangles.

COOKING

The activity of cooking affords many varied opportunities to learn eye-hand coordination: cutting, slicing, grating (use a plastic grater!), spreading and more. It also appeals to the child's senses of sight, smell, taste, touch and hearing, so that all his senses are engaged in this learning experience. Following are some cooking experiences guaranteed to be successful with your child.

TOAST

Be careful when removing toast from toaster.

Materials
toaster
bread
butter
spreads
blunt knife

Method

Help child toast bread. Child spreads butter and spread of his own choice.

FRUIT SALAD

Materials
fruit in season
cream
bowls
beater
blunt knife
peeler

Method

Child peels, slices and dices fruit.

Child beats cream (you can help when he is tired — or stop him before it turns to butter).

He places fruit in bowl, and adds cream.

Enjoy the result together.

PIZZA

Materials
knife for child
olives
ham
other choice goodies (pineapple, prawns, onions)
cabanossi
tomato paste
pita bread (or toast)
cheese
plastic grater

Method

Child slices and dices pizza topping.

He grates cheese and spreads tomato paste on pita bread or toast, then arranges topping.

He then sprinkles with cheese.

You grill pizza.

Have a great lunch!

MAKE-OUR-OWN-BUTTER

Try to keep the rhythm of the shake continuous.

Materials

150 ml (¹/₂ carton) cream
empty jam jar with lid (label removed
    for easy viewing)
bowl
cup

Method

Child pours cream in jar and closes

firmly with lid (with help from you).

She shakes jar up and down —

caution her to hold on tight. Take

turns. Occasionally check consistency

and colour. First cream becomes thick,

then parts into butter and buttermilk.

When butter and milk plop around,

remove lid, strain milk with lid into

cup and empty butter into bowl.

Taste milk, and use butter on toast or

homemade bread. YUM!

MAKING-BUTTER CHANT

'Shake it, shake it, see it part —
We'll make but-ter quick and smart.'

FILM STRIP BOOKMARKS

Very fine needle-work and eye-hand coordination required.

Materials

fine flowers, leaves, dried flowers
unused old film from camera shops
darning/raffia needles
colourful wool
stapler

Method

Child selects flowers/leaves and

arranges them on one film strip.

Place another film strip over it and

staple ends.

Child sews in and out of film holes.

WEAVING

A variation of threading — requiring eye-hand coordination.

Materials
cardboard (13 x 25 cm)
scissors
wool
paper strips
fabric strips

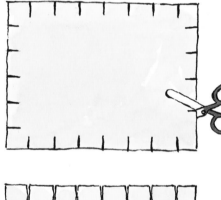

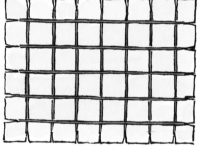

Method

Cut 2 cm parallel incisions on either end of cardboard.

Thread wool tightly, so straight lines of wool are formed.

Tie wool at back of cardboard.

The Game

Child chooses materials and weaves in and out (or over and under).

BE A LETTER

Transposing the shape and form of letters into body shape.

Materials
upper-case letter cards (see p. 26)

Method

Hold up an upper-case letter and ask the child if she can make that shape with her own body. 'Can you make P with your body?'

Start with the first letter of her name. If she does not get the idea, show her how you think you might be able to make the letter with your body.

Ask child to do the rest of the letters in her name. With some letters you might have to add a limb of your own in order to complete it effectively.

HINTS ON CHILDREN'S WRITING

- A good rule to follow with children's writing is to liken it to their speech. Allow it to remain unhindered and organic. Speech and words are not broken up into units of letters and words in the mind of the child. Writing is just another form of speech or communication. So it is best to show the child whole written words and sentences so that it *means* something to him and has a *purpose*.
- Do not drill child, asking him to write the same over and over again — remember that writing must remain fun for the child if he is to want to do it of his own free will. We would not dream of asking a baby to repeat a word over and over again, would we?
- When you write down your child's dictation on a drawing, ask 'what do you want to say?' As time goes on, introduce the concept 'word'. When checking back over the child's dictation, you can ask 'what was the next word?' Mention 'sentence', 'line' and 'letter' in similar contexts. After all, they are also part of speech and communication.
- Write little messages on the blackboard, like 'I love you'. Write his name on the blackboard in a corner and draw a frame around it so it will remain there permanently.

- Draw three equal lines on blackboard and show child how to write foundation script (see p. 109). Emphasise top, middle and bottom part of letters. Ask child to show you where top, middle and bottom is on his body (you may be surprised at the replies you receive). Correct misconceptions. Repeat often as you show how to start letters, how to do the middle bit, and the top (or the other way around, as the case may be).

- If child shows you his writing and tells you what it means — and it is pure fabrication — refrain from rubbishing the effort. Find something to praise. Remember that this is a step in writing as is the babble of a baby prior to speech. Trust the process — it is a fact that children always understand more than they initially express just like a baby who understands you before he can talk. Without hindrances and with encouragement, a child eventually ventures to act out the new skill. All you need to do is to support his developing self-concept in a positive and accepting way.

DRAW A PICTURE
Reinforcing the relationship between the written and spoken word.

Materials
paper
felt pens

Method

Child draws a picture and you write in correct cursive script (p. 109) beneath the drawing what the child dictates to you about the drawing.

Variation

Staple a few pages together and ask your child to draw   pictures for a whole book. Again, she dictates and you write the story.

Read back frequently.

TRACING
Practicing eye-hand coordination and letter shape.

Materials
greaseproof (unwaxed) paper pieces
books with large letters/simple
    pictures
pencils, felt pens
pegs

Method

Child places greaseproof paper over chosen page, holding paper still while copying over letters or pictures.

NB If the child finds it difficult to keep paper still, peg it to the page.

Mathematics

In order for the child to gain a self-confident attitude to the world of numbers, volume, measurement and logic, she needs to have first-hand experience with actual amounts of, say, five apples (the five-ness of apples); with amounts of liquid contained in a cup; with physical distances, with explorations of her surroundings; mind-mapping her known world (a topic also known as topology), which, in a scaled-down form, also includes the fitting together of objects and shapes — keys to key-holes, puzzles, etc.

The activities in this section will help your child gain a solid foundation in mathematical concept formation and understanding.

CONCEPTS

The concepts a child needs to learn in order to grasp higher forms of mathematics are many. Some elementary ones are *more, less, full, empty, same, different, whole, half, numbers, amount, time, many, few, long, short, heavy, light.*

PLAYING WITH NUMBERS

If, during the following games, your child diverts to play with, say, the numerals as people — mummy, daddy, and so on — you can be assured that she is accepting and integrating numbers into her consciousness. If you understand this necessary learning process, you will no longer feel the need to control her play, or get her attention to focus on the game that you thought she needed to learn (like consecutive numbers or similar). When she has explored for a while, you can reintroduce her to the game that you were playing together when she diverted.

SIGNS OF BEGINNING MATHEMATICS

- *attempts to count*
- *notes addition of people or objects*
- *notes missing people or objects*
- *shares*
- *recognizes places he has been before*
- *anticipates arriving at places he has visited before*
- *understands object-to-number as solid (one-to-one correspondence).*

BATHPLAY

If you can't beat them, join them. Rather than telling the children that the bathtub is not a swimming pool, surrender to the fact that bath time is waterplay time. Children learn invaluable mathematical facts from playing with water. Water is familiar to them from their time in the womb and is a kinesthetically pleasurable and calming substance for most children. Knowledge gained includes *full, empty, volume, float, sink, measurement, conservation,* and much more. All you need to do is to provide interesting items for experimentation, and occasionally converse with the child, adding to his vocabulary by naming objects and concepts, and challenging his thinking ('Do you think it will float or sink?').

On different days place the following items in an ice-cream container next to the tub (do not offer child all available material — he will just throw them around, and will not use them with the same focus as when only a few materials are available):

Materials

sponges of different shapes/size/types (try loofah from the chemist)

water-level cans (see following activity)

interesting and safe items that can float and sink. Try, for floating, toy boats, walnut shells, wooden items, corks. And, for sinking, metal lids, keys, small rocks.

funnels of various sizes

various plastic containers

other suggestions are to provide bubbles, natural bath-salt, and food-colouring.

WATER-LEVEL CANS

Does the number or position of the holes effect the water level?

Materials

4 empty 44 g cans
oil paint (bright colours)
hammer and thick nail

Method

Hammer rough edges of cans smooth. Remove labels, and paint. Let dry.

Hammer large holes with thick nail into individual cans as follows:

1 — one hole in centre at bottom of can.

2 — nine holes in centre at bottom of can.

3 — one on side of can, 3 cm below opening.

4 — three holes going down side of can, equally distanced from one another.

Variation

Melt holes into used, clean yoghurt containers instead of using cans.

PLAYDOUGH

Playdough is a tactile substance which seems to comfort and calm children. Playdough lends itself to a variety of mathematical discoveries: mass and its changeability (1 big ball = 10 little balls = 1 big ball again), geometric shapes, weight (one big ball is heavy, one little ball is light). Additionally to its mathematical uses, playdough sets the scene for much imaginary play. It is something that can always be made available.

Here are a variety of recipes to try. Store in refrigerator in an airtight container.

UNCOOKED DOUGH

Materials

1 cup flour
⅓ cup salt
1 tablespoon oil
water
edible dye or food colouring (child chooses colour)
Other optional smells: peppermint essence, vanilla essence, garlic powder, other

Method

Child measures out ingredients with your help and mixes in basin. Help child knead dough well.

Equipment to use with dough

- *roller (ordinary or patterned)*
- *plastic knives*
- *birthday candles*
- *pop sticks*
- *headless matchsticks*
- *cookie cutters*
- *garlic squeezer*
- *potato masher*
- *patty-cake papers*
- *plastic plates*
- *patty-pans*

NB! Offer child only a few of these items each time she plays with the dough so that she can explore the nature of the dough and the equipment without getting over-stimulated.

> 'The most useful rule of education is this: do not save time, but lose it.'
>
> *Jean Jacques Rousseau, Philosopher*

COOKED DOUGH

Materials

1 cup flour
½ cup salt
1 cup water
1 tablespoon oil
2 tablespoons cream of tartar
edible dye or food colouring of child's choice

Method

Heat all ingredients in saucepan until dough leaves side of saucepan.

Turn out on a table and cool.

Knead.

LONGLASTING PLAYDOUGH

Materials

1 cup flour
1 cup boiling water
1 dessertspoon alum (obtain from chemist — safe in small quantities)
1½ cups salt
½ dessertspoon oil
edible dye — child chooses colour

Method

Mix together and knead (as there is hot water, this is an adult's job).

NUMBER HUNT

Matching the written numeral with the actual physical amount.

Method

Using the cards from Bingo game (see p. 27), hunt with the child for clusters of objects; for instance, two cups on a table. Place number 2 card there. (Try no. 6 in a half carton of eggs, and so on.)

LEARNING MATHS BY COOKING

Children's preoccupation with, and pleasure in, food affords us ample opportunities for mathematical concept learning while offering them a cooking experience. You can count the slices of carrots he has cut, discover how many peas are in a pod, note the shapes such as round (circle), oval, the square in a stock-cube . . . *more, less, same, different, big, smaller* . . . little comments including the above help the child verbalise and internalise these difficult concepts in a delicious way. Some cooking ideas are to follow:

CHOCOLATE ICE-CREAM

Materials
150 ml (¹/₂ carton) cream
¹/₃ cup milk
one 55 g egg
2 tablespoons sugar
2 tablespoons cocoa
egg-beater
foil
saucepans
metal spoon
bowl
ice-cube tray with at least 14 cubes,
    or 4 iceblock moulds
halved pop-sticks

Method

Child pours cream and milk into
saucepan. You can scald it.

Child beats egg, sugar and cocoa in
bowl and adds to milk and cream
mixture.

You can place saucepan in a bigger
pan of water and heat and stir until
mixture thickens enough to coat back
of spoon. (Watch out — it splashes!)

Cool saucepan in a bowl of cold
water. Pour mixture into ice-cube
tray. Cover with foil and place in
freezer, turning freezer to maximum.

Let child place halved pop-sticks, one
in each cube, after 1 hour.

After 3 hours cut around edges to free
each cube. Makes 14 delicious cubes.

Variation

Use 4 ice-block moulds instead of the
ice-cube tray.

LUNCH SOUP

Materials
carrot
celery
potato
peas in pods
beans
tomato
bacon
oil
stock cube
peeler
knife
water
pot
blender
number noodles sorted out from
    alphabet noodles

Method

Child washes, peels, slices, and shells
vegetables to best of ability.

You can cook the bacon in a bit of oil
and child can add vegetables,
minding the hot saucepan!

Cover with water and add stock cube.

Bring to boil, then simmer for 20
minutes.

Blend, allowing child to press button.

Serve with pre-cooked number noodles,
and observe the amazing appetite.

GEOMETRIC SHAPE BISCUITS
(ALSO KNOWN AS CHOCOLATE BISCUITS)

Materials
2 cups self raising flour
¹/₂ cup sugar
¹/₂ cup butter
2 dessertspoons cocoa
1 egg
little bit of water if needed for
    consistency
geometric cutters or geometric
    biscuit-sized cardboard shapes and
    blunt knife

Method

Child measures out all ingredients.

Mix and knead.

Roll out so that dough is evenly thin
— this may need your help.

Shapes can be cut with round and
oval biscuit cutters as well as placing
cardboard shapes on top of dough and
cutting around the shape (try triangle,
square).

Place biscuits on tray and bake for 15
minutes in a pre-heated oven at
200°C.

OPTIONAL ICING

Materials

30 g butter
1 cup icing sugar, sifted
2 tablespoons milk
2 tablespoons cocoa

Method

Melt butter.

Add to sifted mixture of cocoa and icing sugar with milk.

Stir to a smooth consistency.

Allow child to apply to cool biscuits with a pastry brush or spread with knife.

A very good sequencing and memory exercise is to ask the child what ingredients you used (first sugar, then milk . . .).

MAKING PUZZLES

If you are not an artist, you can use two identical pictures cut out from posters or magazines. Paste them onto a piece of cardboard and cut one up into jigsaw shapes, tracing the shapes onto the whole picture as a guide for the child. Try finding pictures that interest your child in some way. Puzzles should be no bigger than the drawing paper you give your child.

Puzzles teach logic ('There is a bit of red on this piece, so the next piece must also have some red on it'), and an understanding of parts/wholes and therefore, location in space.

GREETING CARD JIGSAW

Materials
greeting cards
felt pens
scissors

Method

Choose a greeting card — or better still, ask your child to choose one. Divide back of card in jigsaw pattern with felt-pen lines. Child cuts along lines and

reconstructs. (If jigsaw is too squiggly, you will have to do the cutting.)

Variation

When the fridge door gets overcrowded with new pieces of artwork, suggest to child that you make a puzzle of one of his old drawings/paintings by following method above.

COLOUR PUZZLE

Materials
2 identical colour charts from paint
 shop
cardboard
glue
thick black felt pen
clear self-adhesive plastic

Method

Using black felt pen, divide an 18 x 24 cm piece of cardboard into 6 x 6 cm squares. Cut out colour squares from charts — choose strong colours — and glue in centre of each 6 x 6 cm square.

Top: A greeting card with a colourful simple design is ideal.

Middle: On back of the card draw large jigsaw pattern.

Bottom: Child may need assistance cutting.

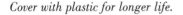

MIX AND MESS

The child's play here will involve concepts such as volume, mass, weight, division, addition and subtraction.

M a t e r i a l s

kitchen scales
basin
large bag of mixed birdseed
spoons
pots
colander
other sandplay equipment

Optional additions to Mix and Mess
macaroni
sand
cooked coloured spaghetti
rice

M e t h o d

Place basin of birdseed on child's table in the garden and watch him have a ball measuring and pouring using kitchen equipment. The birds will eat the leftovers.

S t o r a g e

If you only have dry ingredients (uncooked) you can store Mix and Mess in bucket with tight-fitting lid. NB! Watch that a younger child does not get hold of the dried corn — they tend to try to fit such items into nostrils and other tiny holes! (And watch your 3-year-old, too. Children's actions often take adults by surprise.)

SORTING

Arranging objects according to sameness or colour.

M a t e r i a l s

cutlery
the washing
buttons, shells, nails, screws, pebbles

M e t h o d

Ask child if she would like to help you sort the clean cutlery or washing.

Show child how it is done, and let her help.

Find some shells or pebbles together and help one another sort them into same/different. Apple separators from the greengrocer or egg cartons are useful containers for sorting. Large ice-cube trays could also be useful for small items.

Cover with plastic for longer life.

Repeat process, but do not cover with plastic yet.

Cut out the 16 squares into cards and then cover each with plastic.

T h e   G a m e

Mix up colour cards, and ask child to find the matching one on the board.

V a r i a t i o n

Make an extra set of cards and play Colour Memory (see instructions p. 27).

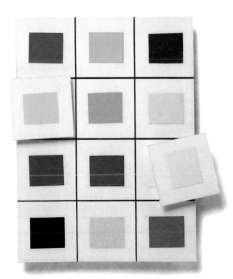

Left: Colour matching puzzle — simple to make, a game for reinforcing colour recognition.

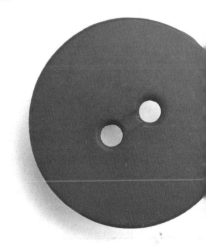

breakfast   lunch

TIME

This is quite a tricky concept to teach small children because they always live in the present time. But physically showing the progression of time will help to make the concept a little easier.

Materials
1 bead
length of wool
child's bookshelf
masking tape

Method

Stretch out wool along length of bookshelf with the bead on it as time marker.

Mark along the shelf certain times, such as breakfast time, morning tea time, lunch time, rest time, Playschool time, and so on, whatever 'time-marks' exist in your household.

Encourage child to move bead along the line as the day progresses.

Once this is established, you can write the daytime hour (see p. 109 for correct number script) on a masking tape which you can insert on the shelf under the wool-line.

Encourage your child to check your digital clock and move bead along the line (using whole hours only) to

number matching the number on the clock.

If you have a traditional clock only, explain to look at the little hand only as that marks the hours of the day. When bead is at the end, the child can move it to the beginning in the morning and start again on a new day.

DOUGH NUMBERS

Measuring and mixing ingredients to model into shapes.

Materials
measuring cup
bowl
1 cup flour
$\frac{1}{2}$ cup salt
water
tactile numbers (see *Feely Letters*, p. 45)

Method

Ask child to fill measuring cup with flour until flour reaches number 1 on cup.

Child pours flour into bowl.

Ask child to fill cup with salt until he reaches '$\frac{1}{2}$' on cup (you can mark with felt pen for extra guidance), and pour into bowl.

Child adds small amounts of water

and mixes and kneads dough with your help until it is pliable.

Child rolls sausages out and makes them into number shapes by looking at number cards, (see Dots-to-numbers-bingo, p. 60).

'Glue' ends and joints together with a bit of water.

Dry out in oven on lowest heat for 2–3 hours. The finished product should be white and slightly soft, hardening when removed from tray to cool.

Offer them to child for painting on another day.

NB! This is not edible dough, and although it will last for a while, it will eventually 'melt'.

Variation

Write out numbers about 8 cm tall and 4 cm wide on greaseproof paper and have child drape sausage directly on top of number shape.

DOTS-TO-NUMBERS-BINGO

Matching actual amount with the numeral.

Materials
two 30 x 20 cm pieces of cardboard
good red or black felt pen
dice

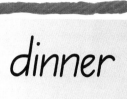

dinner

bedtime

Method

Divide pieces of cardboard into six rectangles, writing neat large numbers '1' to '6' on one side of cardboard, and copy nice big dots just like on dice, from 1 to 6 on the other so that dots and numbers correspond exactly (see p. 109 for correct number script). Repeat with other board.

Cut one of the boards up into cards.

The Game

Hold up a card and ask child to locate it on his board.

When all spaces are filled, shout 'Bingo!'

Variation

Child throws dice.

Counts out dots on dice (with your help).

Finds card with same amount of dots and matches it with correct number on the board (dot-side up).

Shout 'Bingo!' when spaces are all filled.

Extension

Turn board over so that numbers face up, and ask child to have turn with dice.

Ask child to locate correctly dotted card.

Now ask child to turn card around and place it, number up, on matching number on board.

Further Extension

When child has mastered that game, also have cards turned to number side, and ask child to find correct number after throwing dice (he can check on the other side by counting dots).

And/Or

Have ready a container with buttons. Child throws dice and counts out the amount of buttons on the dice, placing them on board instead of card. If you make one more board, you can play this game together.

WHAT'S THE TIME, MR WOLF?

A game involving counting in sequence and taking turns.

Method

This is a game better played with a few children.

You can start by being the wolf.

The children chant 'What's the time Mr Wolf?' and you answer '1 o'clock', '2 o'clock' and so on in numerical order.

Choose what time you want it to be dinner time. You answer 'Dinner time!' when this time is reached, and give chase and catch the child who is then required to sit down upon being caught.

Start the game again.

The last child caught becomes the next Mr Wolf.

Bingo! All the cards have been matched.

MARBLE GAME

Eye-hand coordination and the concept of numbers are practised.

Materials

shoe box
scissors
felt pen
marbles
sultanas (optional)

Method

Cut five holes in shoe box for marbles and write numbers from '1' to '5' above holes.

Place box about 1.5 m away from child and ask her to role marbles into holes.

(Optional) Child receives number of sultanas according to hole entered.

DAYS OF THE WEEK

Variation on the Time activity.

Method

Write the names of each weekday on a piece of cardboard and tape the current day-card to the shelf which marks time (see pp 60, 61).

NUMBER POURING

Coordination of eye-hand are important for accuracy in pouring.

Method

Write neat numbers up the side of a plastic jug. Give child another jug with coloured water (use food colouring) and ask him to pour to number 2 on jug.
Pour back, and ask him to pour to another number.

Variation

Child can throw dice and pour to the number facing up on the dice.

Or

Give child six containers and ask him to pour into one container, two, and so on. This game, too, can be played with dice.

NB. Here again, just a reminder that if the child starts playing an imaginative game with the materials, it is an indication of his integrating the material and making it part of his world. Leave him to play and come back later, suggesting again the more structured game which started off the play, and which you can do together.

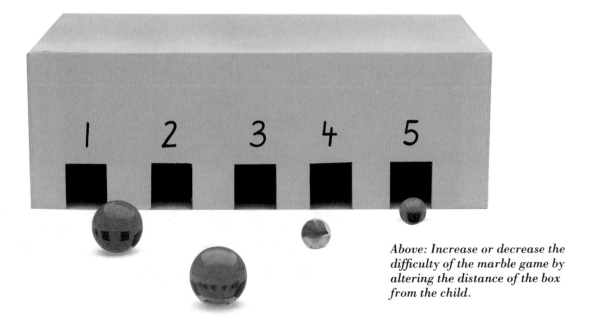

Above: Increase or decrease the difficulty of the marble game by altering the distance of the box from the child.

QUANTITY GAME

Is there more liquid in one of the containers?

Method

Give child a see-through thin, tall container and a wide, short one.

Give him a jug with 1 cup of coloured liquid to pour first into one, then into the other container.

Occasionally ask: 'Has the tall container got more or less in it now than when the water was in the wide one? How did it become more, did you pour more in?' Do not tell him any facts!! Do not belabour the point. Let child experiment with this on his own. Try again in six months, and compare his answers to the previous time.

HOPSCOTCH

Reinforcing counting from numbers 1 to 5 and so on through physical action.

Method

Draw a hopscotch with chalk on the footpath or in the driveway.

Children who cannot hop can jump from square to square. Stay with child for safety.

The rule is that the chalk line must not be stepped on.

Number the squares from 1 to 5. When your child can recognise these numbers you can make a larger hopscotch using all numbers from 1 to 10.

Variation

Mark squares with only uneven numbers (1,3,5,7,9) or with only even numbers (2,4,6,8,10).

Or

Child can throw a pebble into, say, number 5 and hop in all squares until she reaches the pebble, then hop back the same way. You can mark the beginning with the word 'START' and the top with 'FINISH'.

DOT TO DOT SHAPES

Method

Prepare paper with dots that make up geometric shapes: 3 dots for triangle, 4 dots for square, dots for a circle. Child draws lines between dots, completing actual shape.

DOMINO

Domino is an ancient game descended from dice. If you have not yet bought a set of dominoes, now is the time. The game is quite cheap and provides an exciting way of learning numbers.

Method

In the beginning, leave out all dominoes over the number 4 and otherwise follow the rules.

Do not bother counting how many points are left over in someone's hand.

End the game with the person able to lay all his dominoes down.

When child has learned the game and can play well with dominoes up to number 4, introduce remaining dominoes, explaining how they look, and counting the numbers with the child. Then, following the rules, continue with the game.

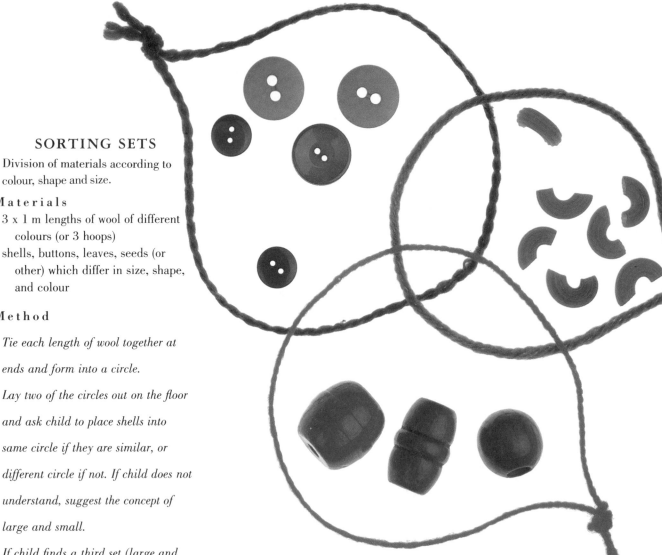

SORTING SETS

Division of materials according to colour, shape and size.

Materials

3 x 1 m lengths of wool of different colours (or 3 hoops)

shells, buttons, leaves, seeds (or other) which differ in size, shape, and colour

Method

Tie each length of wool together at ends and form into a circle.

Lay two of the circles out on the floor and ask child to place shells into same circle if they are similar, or different circle if not. If child does not understand, suggest the concept of large and small.

If child finds a third set (large and pink/small and pink, for instance), place third circle between the two circles so it overlaps them both.

SCRAMBLED NUMBERS

Reorganising mixed-up numbers into numerical order.

Method

Using your number cards (see p. 65), lay them out in order from 1 to 10 and read from left to right. Read again, and encourage child to read with you.

Now ask child to close eyes as you swap around two numbers.

Ask child to open eyes and guess what is different. Ask child to place numbers back where they belong.

This is a fun game which you can play many times. Leave intervals of weeks in between, so that the game remains fun rather than a chore.

WEIGHING GAME

It's fun to experiment with the unpredictability of volume and weight.

Materials
scales
objects to weigh

Method

Ask child to feel the weight of an object. Ask child to feel the weight of another object (try a feather).

Ask which one feels heavier (show by straining face, voice and body to illustrate the meaning of 'heavy').

Variation

When child is accustomed to the concept of comparing weights, introduce kitchen scales and weigh items to check which item weighs more.

Or

Provide child with 1 kg or 2 kg items to weigh; a 1 kg bag of flour, for example. Check weight on scales and compare to declared weight on item.

Or

Ask child to draw a picture of each member of the family. Ask child who she thinks is the lightest and who weighs the most.

Ask family to weigh themselves and write their weight in kilograms under each drawing.

Or

Measure height of each person in your family and record on the back of a door or wherever appropriate. Talk about who is tallest, shortest, taller than, shorter than.

Or

When playing with playdough, weigh playdough.

Roll sausages.

Weigh first one sausage and then all sausages.

Compare the weights.

ALL NUMBERS BINGO

Matching and collating all forms of expressing numbers.

Method

Prepare board and cards as for Bingo *(see p. 27), writing numerals, names of numbers, and number-dots on boards and cards, i.e. four, 4,::).*

GEOMETRIC SHAPE DRAWING

Use different shapes as base for child's own art work.

Method

Cut out large geometric shapes (circles, triangles, squares) and leave them on your child's table for her to draw on.

Variation

Draw smaller geometric shapes (circle on one piece of paper, triangle on another, square on another) for your child, and encourage her to include them somehow in her own drawing.

Or

Draw many circles, triangles and squares on nice colourful paper and provide child with good children's scissors (from toy shop). Child can cut along line of shapes.

Provide child with paste and pieces of paper.

Child pastes shapes onto paper.

Or

When child has become familiar with these shapes, provide rectangles, ovals, diamonds, pentagons, hexagons and stars.

Or

Play Geometric Shape Memory Game *(see p. 27) with 24 cards.*

Neatly cut out six each of circles, squares, triangles and diamonds from colourful paper and glue onto cards. Children love this game.

As child improves, add more and more items until she is adding up to 10.

DIVISION

Place three plastic animals (or dolls or teddies or cars) on table.

Cut up an apple into six pieces and ask child to feed the animals so that each one has as many pieces as the other.

Try up to five plastic animals and 10 pieces of apple) over a period of time.

Or

Ask child how many pieces of bread she would like her sandwich to be. While she watches, cut sandwich diagonally (two triangles) or on another day diagonally twice (four triangles). You can also make two rectangles or four squares.

If you feel really creative, cut all four corners off to make a circle sandwich. (Dare we add that you can halve it, too?)

WATER LEVEL GAME

A problem solving activity — if this happens then . . .

Materials

2 large drawings of a glass tipping
    45° on two separate sheets of paper
glass half-filled with coloured water
    (add food colour)

OPERATION GAME

Practicing skills of observation and concepts of subtraction, addition and division.

Materials

5 objects, such as plastic animals, keys, apple, biscuits, tissues, dolls bread

Method

SUBTRACTION

Line up objects and 'read' them with the child from left to right.

Repeat.

Ask child to close eyes while you remove one object.

Ask child to open eyes and guess what is missing (leave space empty where object has been removed as a reminder).

Take turns to hide objects.

Make it harder by hiding 2, then 3 objects as child gets the idea of the game.

ADDITION

Start with three objects. Ask child to close eyes while you add an object.

Ask child to open eyes and guess what is different.

Method

Ask child to look at glass. 'Do you see the coloured water? Show me with your finger where the top of the water is. Now, I am going to tip the glass so that I can pour the water but before I do, I want you to think about what the water will look like when I tip the glass. Can you draw the water line on this drawing of a glass which is tipping?'

Present child with drawing. Child will draw water-level.

Now ask child to observe water level as you tip glass over sink.

Give child the other drawing of glass and ask him to draw what he has seen.

Ask child to guess how water level will look when glass stands on table again.

Ask child if he thought the water would look like it did: 'Were you surprised?' Do not tell child facts if he has not observed correctly! (Yes, it's hard to keep quiet!)

Try again in 6 months.

MAZE GAME

Each path is about the same length but they do not lead to the same place...

Materials

3 different coloured chalk

Method

Draw two houses with chalk, spacing them about 3 m apart, on the concrete outside, or on the footpath. Using three different-coloured chalks, draw three lines from one house's door, but with only one line leading to the other house's door, and the other two ending elsewhere.

The Game

Ask child to walk along lines and find the line which leads from Little Red Ridinghood's house to Grandmother's house.

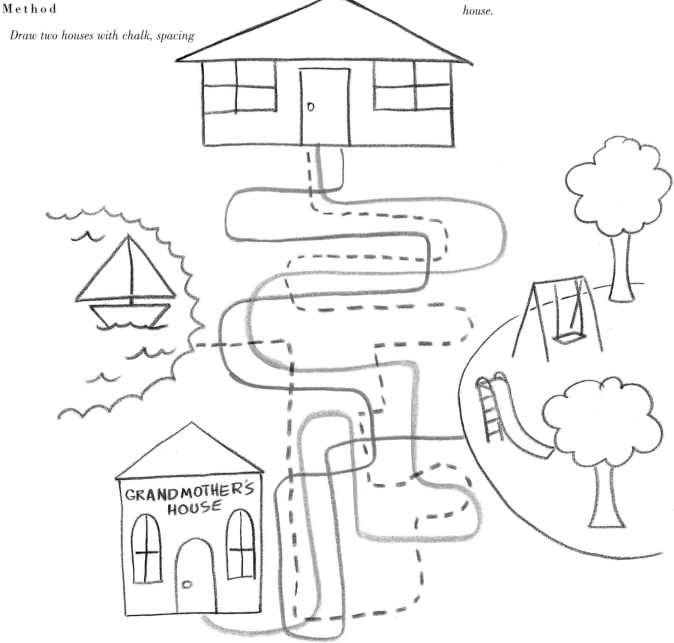

GRANDMOTHER'S HOUSE

HOW LONG IS 100

For the older child to physically
discover that counting involves volume.

Materials

adding machine roll
pencil

Method

*Give child the roll (which is
surprisingly cheap!) and announce, 'I
thought we would have a look at how
long 100 is. Would you like to try
that?' Tell child that all he has to do
is to write all the numbers on the roll
from 1 to 100, and he can use as
much of the paper as he wants to. It is
a good idea to have him write it on
the floor to provide the space for the
unwinding roll. Most children find
this a fascinating game, and it really
gives them a sense of the amount
because of all the writing they are
doing. You can be around to remind
the child what comes after 29 or some
other difficult junction of numbers. If
he needs to be reminded of how
numbers look or which way they turn,
write numbers up on the blackboard or
lay out number cards (p. 65) for him
to follow.*

NEIGHBOURHOOD MAP

A fun way to observe and actually map
out the child's immediate environment.

Materials

sheet of cardboard
thick felt pen

Method

*Draw your local streets on cardboard.
Locate on the map where your home
should be, and child can draw house
there, and also other familiar
landmarks such as friends' houses,
shops and trees.*

*Child can use map to drive toy cars
on or walk dolls on.*

Variation

*Draw a smaller version, and go out
one day, following the map.
Discover new streets and add onto
map.*

CALCULATOR GAMES

If you want your child to continue his
fascination with numbers, give him a
cheap calculator. Here are some
calculator games you can play:

- *Suggest to child that he presses a
  number. Then ask him to press C
  and see it disappear.*

- *Suggest to child to press 1, then –,
  and then 1 again. Ask him to try it
  by himself.*

- *Suggest to child to press 1, then +,
  then 1 again. 'What's changed?' Ask
  him to try it by himself.*

- *Ask him to press a number you have
  drawn from number cards (see
  p. 65). Repeat above without you
  looking at number. Guess his
  number. Take turns.*

- *Encourage child to play with, and
  explore, calculator in his own way.*

MULTIPLICATION BINGO

This activity is suitable only for an older child, as it involves the complex concept of multiplication.

Materials

cardboard, 30 x 20 cm
thick felt pen

Method

Make two boards for each table as follows: Divide boards into 10 equal rectangles. Write the answer to multiplication in a jumbled way (not in order) on each rectangle. For instance, if it is the five-times table, write in each rectangle as follows:

10,25,5,50, and so on. The back of each board must correspond exactly with the front. In those rectangles write the multiplication (5 x 10 on the back of 50, and so on).

Cut one board up into cards, retaining the other as the board.

Teaching only one table at a time, tell child the multiplication and the answer (the correct mathematical term for 'answer' is product*). Repeat.*

Now give child board with answers up and show each card, one at a time. He is to take card and place it on the correct answer on the board.

At the end, ask child to check his answer by turning around each card and verifying answer with number beneath it on the board.

When he seems to have mastered it, ask him to time himself and to write down how many seconds he takes to fill the board correctly.

Repeat while child enjoys it.

Turn board over so that the multiplication faces upwards and show cards with answers. Child can time himself until table is learnt.

Variation

Make a Memory game (see p. 27) of 20 cards by writing out two of each of multiplication and answer on each card (for example, 4 x 4 = 16).

Or

Write out 10 cards with the multiplication, and 10 cards with the answer. Child has to find and correctly match both in order to gain a pair.

Art

RECIPE FOR PAINT AND PASTE

We learn to think creatively through the tool of imagination, a unique and human gift. Learning to think creatively is what the adults of tomorrow must do if they are to rectify our many mistakes. The past cannot give us all the answers, and so it makes little sense to teach children exclusively what we know.

The use of language is one very important way of teaching our children to think creatively: allowing children to talk and express authentically; teaching children, through our own involvement, to love reading and writing and communicating.

Another excellent way of fostering creativity is through artistic expression and experimentation. The activities on the next few pages are designed for the pre-school child, and will open many doors to colours, textures and possibilities. Additionally, childrens' art is inextricably tied up with skills in eye-hand co-ordination and fine motor movements — essential skill-builders for a child who is learning to write.

Signs of creativity
- *is curious*
- *takes things apart*
- *has a flexible attitude, willing to try new experiences*
- *finds new uses for things*
- *daydreams*
- *makes up stories and games*
- *enjoys art activities*

Materials

3 tablespoons cornflour or starch
water
edible dye

Method

Make a runny paste from cornflour and cold water.

Pour in boiling water rapidly while stirring vigorously as if making a sauce, until consistency is creamy and free of lumps. This is the paste.

If you are going to use the paste for paint, simply add dye.

It will keep for about a week in an airtight container in the refrigerator.

Variation

If you keep getting lumps in the paste try reversing the method by adding the paste to the boiling water while stirring.

Alternate Uses: *Fingerpaint and footpaint.*

WATERPAINT

Add edible dye to water until mixture reaches a vibrant colour.

DYES

Use only non-toxic edible powder paints — the brand we used is called 'Edicol'. Dyes are available from toyshops or pre-school equipment suppliers. Use the ratio of a quarter of a teaspoon of dye to one cup of paste.

Food colours, readily available from supermarkets, can also be used, although they are not as bright.

THE USE OF GLUE

Glue is used to stick objects heavier than paper. The use of glue, preferably woodwork glue, must be a supervised activity. You can use a small container for glue, and a pop stick for application. Explain to child that only a tiny amount is necessary to make things stick, unlike paste.

DYE FOR PRINTING

Water down paste consistency until almost watery and add double the amount of dye that you would use for paint.

PAPER

You can buy coloured paper at an arts and crafts shop. White paper can be obtained from the newsagent in a block which resembles typing paper. If you cannot get the above, use computer paper, butchers' paper or used architects' paper.

Right: Allow your child to express her ideas and emotions creatively.

DYED MACARONI AND RICE

Materials

edible dyes
macaroni with holes or rice
containers (margarine or ice-cream)
water
baking trays
oil
sieve

Method

Make up strong cold dye solutions (water-colours) in containers.

Make up as many different colours as needed.

Add macaroni or rice. Leave briefly and then drain.

Spread macaroni or rice on lightly-oiled trays so that each piece is separate.

Leave to dry and re-harden.

Store in containers.

Uses

Making necklaces; gluing on its own or in collage.

COLOURED SAND, SAWDUST, WOOD SHAVINGS

Materials

edible dye
margarine or other similar containers
sand, sawdust, wood shavings,
    headless matchsticks
newspapers

Method

Make up red, blue, yellow, green or other colour dye solutions. Half-fill containers with dye.

Add sand, sawdust and other materials. Stir.

Leave overnight.

Empty contents onto thick layer of newspaper and spread evenly.

Allow to dry thoroughly.

Pour back into containers for future use.

Uses

Gluing onto cardboard on its own or in collage.

EASELS

An easel can be purchased at a large toy shop or the toy section of department stores.

Or

Two bulldog clips can be secured horizontally about 30 cm apart onto your wooden fence, a back door, or some other acceptable place. The clips should be approximately 1.2 m from the ground. A sheet of painting-sized paper (about 50 x 70 cm) can be clipped into place, ready for the activity.

PAINT CONTAINERS

Large used yoghurt containers make good paintpots.

The best size for most purposes is about 15 x 25 cm. Sometimes a large piece of paper seems to defeat a child, much like a dinner plate piled high with food.

SCISSORS

These need special mention. They should be of very good quality, and sharp. The blunt variety is acceptable for use when child is not constantly supervised, but it is important not to frustrate a beginner cutter at serious work with hopeless scissors — the child already has eye-hand coordination to master! The small dressmaking type scissors with one or both corners rounded are excellent for the purpose. But do watch the child while she is working with these scissors!

An easy method of learning to cut is to place the child's index and middle finger in the second hole of the scissors. A child's hand is not yet strong enough to use only two fingers at the beginning. You can also help by holding the paper taut which she is cutting.

PAINT VARIATIONS

Materials

- paste + dye
- water + dye
- acrylic paints (non-toxic), available in tubes or bottles at art supply shops or stationery outlets
- add sand to paint for gritty effect
- add container with collage materials (see p. 74) which child can stick onto painting as work progresses.

BRUSHES

The child could be using up to six colours in one session. Ideally you will need one brush for each colour. Quality No. 8 and No. 10 brushes with 1 cm-thick round wooden shafts are a worthwhile investment.

The brush hair on these are made from animal bristle or quality nylon, tightly bound, and with a rather thick and bushy appearance. Brushes such as these can be purchased in good toy or artist supply outlets and will outlast you child's early childhood years.

You can also add other brush thicknesses, and even 'real' paint brushes for a variety of experiences with this medium. Thin brushes can be used for water painting. Try the shaving brush one day for a fun medium. For pasting, a pastry brush is ideal.

HOW SHOULD A CHILD PAINT?

Remind child often to wipe brush before painting. Point out how paint runs down the paper and ruins her intentions if brush is not wiped properly. If child pushes brush right into paper, show her how to wipe it gently along the paper instead. Demonstrate how to hold brush (like holding a pencil) occasionally, but do not insist. She will eventually learn this, and if you make an issue of it, the child may lose interest in painting altogether.

Allow the child to paint as much or as little as she wants to — do not insist on the whole paper being filled in. If, however, the child paints one line and then requests a new piece of paper you can suggest that she paint some more on the same paper first.

Until around four years of age most children do not draw or paint anything which resembles a known object. Prior to this age children are basically experimenting with colour and their own control over the brush. Upon mastery of the latter, the thoughts and the actions of the hand start cooperating, and the child will begin to symbolise what she sees. Usually, the self (or a person) emerges as the first symbol. Later, the sun, and a beautiful little rainbow. And what is more important to a person than the self, and what more important to self than life-giving sun, and rainbows of beauty! The process is fascinating.

THE IMPORTANCE OF ENCOURAGEMENT

Avoid showing the child how to draw or paint some object unless child actually requests this of you. Let the child find her own way of expression. In art nothing is correct or incorrect; art is an inner language finding outer expression.

Adults tend to draw the typical childish line drawing of house, sun, stick-figure or tree for the child to copy. But this type of drawing is not humanly inherent — it can be likened to speaking only one-word sentences to a baby. Take the child to the art gallery one day, instead.

Children are very sensitive to expectations and to their own limited abilities, so it is best to underplay your expectations rather than fully expressing them. A hurtful and destructive correction often overheard is, 'But where is the door (or arms, or . . .)?' when a proud child presents his first few paintings of a house, or some other 'real' object. No doubt the parent wishes to teach, to make the child aware of an omission. But symbolic representation takes a developmental course and cannot (and ought not) be hurried along. Eventually the child begins to paint the door, the wheels on the car, the arms on the person. Allow the child to discover as you too discovered — hopefully unaided.

Often, too, children will paint for the sake of mixing colours and experimentation. Try to avoid questioning your child about what each painting represents. Chances are that the child will see an accidental image in the painting and tell you 'it's a snake', or some other rationalisation in order to satisfy your query. Questioning may also cause her to assume that you expect the painting to look like some-

COLLAGE

These are only suggestions of materials to use, experiment with others.

Materials

bits of coloured paper	cardboard shapes, rolls, tubes, cylinders
milk bottle tops	
leather	glue
bits of wood	paste (you can add dye sometimes)
wood shavings	
sawdust	scissors
sand	large sheets of paper
cardboard boxes	
macaroni	hessian
natural resources such as leaves, bark and seeds	paint
	crayons
	cardboard
buttons	felt pens
bits of fabric	
shells	

Method

Prepare various red collage items.

Offer child white cardboard to paste onto.

Variation

Have different white items prepared.

Offer child red cardboard to paste onto.

Or

Offer various textures for collage regardless of colour such as:

hard and soft

smooth and rough

bumpy and furry

and any of the above combinations

These items could include fabrics, hessian, sandpaper, bark and seeds,

thing. The child may therefore feel inadequate because she cannot yet produce such works of art, and that would defeat the purpose behind offering the opportunity to experiment with different artistic media. Experimentations with colour mixing should not be underestimated, as such work is pure scientific investigation and the groundwork for experience and more expert experimentation and knowledge. Mixing of colours also leads to expectations and predictions, a requirement for basic mathematics and logic, reading, and other such foundation stones of a developing mind.

Right: Allow your child to express himself with the different medium — this is an example of types of Be prepared to see abstract pictures.

papers (cellophane, crêpe), string, twine, wool, cottonwool balls

O r

Precut geometric shapes, such as circles, squares, triangles, rectangles, ovals, diamonds, and more.

WOOL AND FABRIC COLLAGE

Wool and fabric will require a slightly stronger glue than paper.

Materials

bits of various coloured wool and/or
  fabric pieces
glue
cardboard

Method

Child chooses wool or fabric and glues onto card in desired pattern.

LINE CUTTING

Make sure the scissors are sharp enough to cut cleanly.

Materials

pre-drawn straight lines on paper
  with 1–2 cm gaps to make strips
  when cut out
scissors
paste
coloured paper squares

Method

Ask child to cut strips by following the line on the paper (see Scissors, p. 72). Child pastes completed cut-outs on coloured paper as a contrast.

Variation

Could also use child's art or cards. Child pastes one end of paper strip and curls the other end so it overlaps, forming a ring or link. Threads next strip through first link. Repeats procedure, making a chain.

O r

Draw circles, squares, triangles and diamonds on paper. Child cuts along line of pre-drawn shapes and pastes on coloured or plain paper.

CUTTING AND PASTING

Here the child cuts his own pieces to attach to his collage.

Materials

scissors
old magazines
old greeting cards
paste
cardboard or paper

Method

Child cuts out pictures from old magazines or cards and pastes on cardboard or paper.

FOIL/CELLOPHANE PAINTING

Try limiting and varying the medium used for collage making.

Materials

20 x 20 cm foil/cellophane
thin brushes
acrylic paints
cardboard/coloured paper
glue

Method

Child paints on foil or cellophane using thin brushes, and then glues onto contrast such as coloured square, or cardboard.

Variation

If using cellophane, display on window as is.

BLOCK STAMPS

A variety of textures and shapes on wood blocks are a great way to create new images.

Materials

wooden blocks (free leftovers at timberyard)
sandpaper
paint (optional)
drawer handle knobs, one for each stamp
glue
printing dye
styrofoam tray lined with sponge
paper
Items to print: sponge cut to form circle, square, diamond and triangle; string wound around; popsticks; corduroy; bark; hessian; textured lino; dough letters or numbers or other.

Method

Smooth blocks with sandpaper. Dust and paint (optional).

Glue printing object on one flat side, screwing in knob on the other.

Prepare printing dye in styrofoam tray lined with sponge, and offer stamps to child.

The Game

Child can stamp on large sheets of paper. Offer some of the stamps on one day, others on another day.

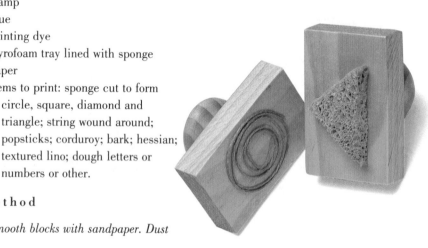

Above: Smooth drawer knobs attached to block stamps make them easy to handle.

LEMON AND APPLE PRINTING

Shapes from the natural environment recreated.

Materials

2 apples
2 lemons
2 polystyrene trays (or other containers) lined with sponge
2 dye solutions
paper

Method

A few hours before activity, cut one apple and one lemon in half lengthways through centre, and the other pair sideways through centre, so two distinct patterns in fruit appears.

Prepare meat trays with sponges soaked with dye.

Try a few prints yourself to check dye and offer it to child.

Child will print and perhaps discover the two distinct patterns in fruit halves.

POTATO PRINTING

It is best initially for an adult to cut shapes out of the potato.

Materials

potatoes
knife
styrofoam meat tray or other flat
    container
sponge
dye (see p. 70)
paper

Method

Halve potatoes. Cut out shape in potato — an older child can scratch on their own shape and cut out around it, or dig shape out, but you may have to do it for a younger child yourself.

Line tray with sponge and pour on dye solution.

Child presses potato into sponge, then prints firmly onto paper.

NB A good printing hint is to place an old blanket under the work for a better print. You can cover blanket with newspaper.

Right: Try varying the cut pattens, they can be images or geometric shapes.

Above: A variety of fruits can be used for printing — a disposable medium.

TISSUE STRIPS

Remind the child to use small amounts of glue on the strips.

Materials
  white paper
  4 cm tissue paper strips of various colours
  paste

Method

Child pastes strips of tissue paper onto white background, allowing strips to overlap.

DYED SERVIETTES

An activity involving the mathematical concept of division.

Materials
  paper serviettes (plain)
  paper towel sections
  doilies
  3 primary water colours (red, blue, yellow)
  containers
  clothes horse/line
  coloured paper
  paste

Method

Fold serviette (or paper towel or doily) in half, and half again to form a square (except doily).

Cut corners away.

Dip edges into same or different dyes.

Dry on clothes horse or line.

Gently open and glue onto contrasting coloured paper somewhat larger than serviette.

SUGARED CHALK

A different medium/texture for the child to use when drawing.

Materials
  coloured chalk — do not use dustless chalk for this activity as it melts in water
  margarine container half-filled with very hot water
  1 tablespoon sugar
  paper (white, black and coloured for this activity)

Method

Place chalk (half sticks will do) into container.

Add sugar, stir, and leave to cool.

Child selects desired colours as she needs them and draws on paper, placing chalk sticks back into the water when finished.

Chalk will not rub off as it normally does, due to the sugar, and the colours are much brighter.

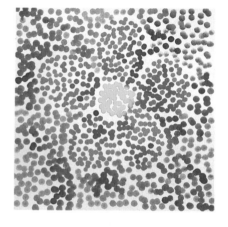

COTTONBUD PAINTING

Use a variety of materials to paint with – other than paintbrushes.

Materials
  red, blue and yellow water colour
  small containers
  cottonbuds
  paper

Method

Arrange small containers, such as egg cups, with colours and buds.

Child uses buds like paintbrushes, replacing them in their own container each time after painting.

The results are beautiful paintings, because of the precision and absorbent nature of the buds.

CRAYON/WAX AND WATER-PAINT

A magical way to discover the water resistant effect of crayons.

Materials
ends of candles or whole wax-based
    chunky crayons.
paper
water-paint
brush

Method

Child draws a picture with candles or crayons and then paints all over paper with water-paint.

PUNCHING

An activity involving small muscle dexterity.

Materials
plain or coloured paper shapes
Sellotape
hole punch
cellophane (various colours)
paste

Method

Child tapes two matching shapes together lightly, and punches holes all over or however he wants to.

Separates shapes and pastes cellophane on one, and then pastes matching shape over cellophane.

It can be displayed on the window.

CARDS FOR SPECIAL DAYS

Creating something special to carry a written message.

Materials
lightweight cardboard
felt pens
paste
various artwork

Method

Fold cardboard like a card.

Child cuts out a piece of her previous work and glues it onto the front of the card.

Child dictates a message which you write inside the card (see p. 109).

Child signs own name if she can.

Variation

Artwork can be worked straight onto the cardboard. Suggestions are: rubbing (see p. 80), water-paint picture, fruit printing (see p. 76), cottonbud painting, a felt pen drawing. Or a fine felt pen can be used for a delicate picture. Certainly the cards will be original and beautiful.

Uses

Mother's Day, Father's Day, Christmas, birthdays, invitations, or other special occasions.

MASKING TAPE PAINTING

Use strong/thick paper to avoid tearing the art when removing tape

Materials
masking tape
paper
scissors
small roller from hardware store or
    supermarket
waterpaint
sponge
styrofoam tray or rectangular take-
    away container

Method

Child cuts pieces of masking tape and places them on paper in chosen pattern.

You soak sponge in waterpaint and place in styrofoam container.

Child rolls roller over sponge and all over paper.

Let dry, and then pull off strips of tape carefully and admire results.

PIZZA PICTURES

Not all creative work needs to be kept; experiment with different materials.

Materials

small round basin
paper circles large enough to cover bottom of basin
various colours of acrylic paint (or cornflour-based paint, reasonably runny)
marbles (NB Remove these after use — they are too tempting to pop in mouth)
container with clean water.

Method

Child places paper in bottom of basin.

Spoons colours in small amounts onto paper and adds marbles.

Holds basin with two hands and wriggles it so that marbles run through colours, making tracks.

Clean marbles in water container before next picture.

Variation

Try golf balls.

GLUE PRINTING

The skills needed to cut, paste and sprinkle are practiced.

Materials

paper
scissors
paste
sawdust

Method

Child cuts out own or pre-drawn shape from paper.

Paints glue all over shape, and then places it on paper, pressing firmly.

Peels off shape quickly, and sprinkles sawdust over sticky spot on paper. Dusts off.

Variation

Use sand instead of sawdust. (See p. 72 on how to dye these materials.)

Or

Paint child's foot/hand with glue. Print, following directions above.

Or

Paint flat objects with glue and follow directions above.

Try shoes, boots, pegs or gadgets from the kitchen drawer.

RUBBING

Attach the object to the surface with blu-tack to keep it from moving.

Materials

assorted fruit/vegetable nets with large and small holes
paper
waxed-based crayons
edible dye
waterpaint

Method

Child places fruit net under paper and rubs crayons over paper. Crayon used upright or flat on paper produce different effects — the flat method yields best results.

Use various nets with different sized holes and change crayon colours one after the other for interesting results.

Variation

Paint over pattern with water-based edible dye. Crayon markings will stand out.

Or

Place other objects beneath paper for rubbing, such as scissors, flat graters, geometric shapes, cotton reel ends, Lego, corrugated cardboard (or just cardboard from a box), doilies, shells, coins, leaves, patterned wallpaper, and any other objects which are flat with a raised surface.

Or

Use leftover candle ends instead of crayons and paint over with water-paint for a mystery picture.

CELLOPHANE AND TISSUE STRIPS

For the older child as the activity can be quite fiddly with the strips and glue.

Materials

cardboard cut with window in centre (as a frame)

2 cm wide strips of tissue paper and/ or cellophane of various colours — the length of strips should be somewhat longer than window in cardboard

paste

Method

Child applies paste to frame and sticks on strips overlapping one another.

WET PAPER PAINTING

Use the water sparingly — coat the page lightly.

Materials

newspaper

wet sponge

paper

strong waterpaint solutions in various colours (try filling sections of ice-cube tray with different colours)

thin brushes or cotton buds

Method

Spread layer of newspaper on table.

Gently sponge water on paper laid out on newspaper, so that it glistens.

Child paints on wet paper. Dry flat on newspaper.

DOILIES

Suitable for older children, to practice small muscle skills.

Materials

scissors
pre-folded paper
coloured paper squares
sieve
water-paint
nailbrush or washing-up brush

Method

Child cuts into fold at intervals, then turns paper and cuts at an angle until two cuts meet and a bit of paper is cut off. Opens paper and pastes onto coloured paper square for a fine effect.

Or

Pre-fold different shapes (squares, circles, triangles).

Or

Use doilies for rubbing activity (see Rubbing p. 80).

Or

Lie doily flat on white paper and place a metal sieve upside down over doily.

Child dips nailbrush or washing-up brush into water-paint and brushes sieve all over until the droplets of paint are brushed off.

Lift off sieve and doily.

Let spatter painting dry.

NB! This is a messy activity, so choose clothes and workspace accordingly.

'The young child paints and draws what he feels and what is meaningful to him . . . For example, the head is more important and therefore he gives it greater relative size . . . than the body. He also uses colours imaginatively . . . a cat can be green; a house purple; a person's hair, blue.'

Frank and Theresa Caplan, Authors of 'The Power Of Play'

ANIMAL TEMPLATES

Requires developed concentration and small muscle skills.

Materials

old magazines
cardboard
paste

Or

discarded baby's board book of
    animals
white paper
crayons
paste
contrasting coloured paper

Method

*Find pictures of animals and cut out
or draw your own and cut out.*

Glue onto cardboard and allow to dry.

Cut around animal shape.

*Child places animal template on white
paper.*

*Child traces around the shape —
show how to hold a template still on
the paper with one hand while tracing
all around it with the other.*

*Child colours animal with crayons,
and cuts around outline.*

*Pastes onto contrasting coloured
paper.*

Or

*Child uses self for template. Child
traces hands and feet. You can trace
his profile or around his body.*

TEXTURED ANIMAL SHAPES

Trace around shapes, cut out then glue on scrunched crêpe balls.

Materials

small animal templates (see *Animal
    Templates*, above)
white paper
strips of crêpe paper
paste

Method

*Child traces around chosen animal
shape.*

*Show child how to roll little balls of
crêpe paper between thumb, index and
middle fingers.*

*Child glues crêpe balls inside animal
shape when he has sufficient balls.*

*He may get tired of making too many
little balls — let him make as few or
as many as he wishes.*

Above: *Although creatively
restrictive these activities provide
valuable use of fine hand movements
and an opportunity for the child to
follow instructions.*

Cut out diamond shape and reinforce corners before punching the holes.

Decorate tail with coloured materials and attach to one corner of kite.

KITE

This kite is a bright decoration for the display board.

Materials

large sheet of paper — used architect
  paper is a good strong medium
scissors
masking tape
string/wool
crayons or paint

Method

Pre-draw large diamond shape on

paper.

Child cuts out diamond shape.

Punch hole near one of the corners

and reinforce with masking tape.

Tie length of string through hole.

If desired punch another hole and

attach wool and fabric tail. Child

decorates kite.

DECORATED MILK CARTONS

Use a strong glue to paste paper to carton or result may be disappointing.

Materials

4 strips of paper,
    each 19.5 x 7 cm
felt pens
paste
milk cartons
string
stapler
can
hammer
paper

Method

Child draws on all four strips of paper and glues onto sides of carton. Place string/wool inside opening of carton and staple together. Press down so only sides are visible. Hang as mobile.

Or

Using a can, smooth opening with hammer. Offer child paper the size of tin (like a label). Child draws on it as above or uses art methods as for Cards for Special Days *(p. 79). Glue around tin and use as pencil holder.*

Above: The child can recycle household items and decorate to make pieces of art that can also be used.

Body Skills — Physical Agility

Physical agility is sometimes called Gross Motor Ability. The active ingredients for physical activities are freedom of movement and opportunity to experiment. The ancients knew that physical agility was an important part of education. Physical prowess and confidence is part and parcel of the building of a positive self-esteem in the child. Physical education in the early childhood years ought to be fun, supportive, and most importantly, non-competitive: children, who are learning body balance with a constantly changing and growing body, learning body- and space-awareness and physical possibility and ability, can become frozen in their learning if fear of failure through competitive sports is a reality in their lives.

Another block to growth is the too-careful, over-protective approach. Safety is certainly a factor, and in order to provide the child with relative safety, opportunity and freedom a fine balance has to be reached, and constantly adjusted, as the child grows more able. Emphasis should be given to experimentation, exploration, and permission to enjoy for the sake of enjoyment, rather than for any expected outcome. Given plenty of opportunities, a child will gain eye–hand coordination, eye–foot coordination, a love of his body, and retain his untainted boldness and admirable courage to conquer the new.

Research has shown that children who are exposed to the learning of physical skills earlier than others do not necessarily learn it better — physical unfolding of ability is developmental in the early years, and thus to a large extent unchangeable. However, for balance of development, children need appropriate opportunity and encouragement to safely explore their abilities in the physical world.

The following pages will provide you with simple aids to make, and many activities which will help to foster your child's body-awareness and expression.

SIGNS OF GROWING BODY SKILLS

- *attempts new skills*
- *is physically active*
- *moves in a natural and free manner*
- *acts frustrated until new skill is mastered*

ROLLING GAMES

A good rule about balls is to provide a large ball for a small child, and a small ball for a large child. A 15–20 cm diameter ball of foam or soft vinyl is a good size for the early years.

Method

Sit opposite child with open legs (like a V) towards each other.

Roll ball to child. Child rolls ball back upon receiving it.

The legs act as walls to prevent ball from straying.

BALLOON PLAY

Small children love balloons and should be given many opportunities to throw, catch, kick and bounce them. Balloons are a soft and slow version of a ball. Sometimes children get frightened of balls because a hard ball has hit them unexpectedly. Balloon play can help restore their confidence.

Right: Playing provides a great opportunity for children to socially interact while developing physical skills.

CATCH THE BUBBLES

A fun eye-hand-body coordination game.

Materials

margarine container
soap flakes
boiling water
straws
other items which have holes for
   bubble blowing — try potato masher
   or bent wire

Method

Dissolve soap flakes with small amount of boiling water and let cool. With a straw or other items, blow bubbles for the child and encourage him to chase and catch them. Take turns blowing and catching.

CLIMBING

Children are natural climbers. If you can go for a holiday to a mountainous area (and you do not already live in one), go for a mountain climbing walk. You will be amazed as your eighteen-months-old toddler outdoes you with joy! If you have a ladder and a backyard, use it to the child's advantage whenever you can fully supervise her. You can:

- *lie ladder flat on ground (secure ends with tentpegs) for child to scramble along, climb along and, with your help, walk along.*

- *raise ladder slightly onto two bricks lying side by side at both ends, and repeat above.*

- *lean ladder towards a low object like a chair. Secure. Encourage child to climb ladder.*

- *if you have a stepladder, place in secure spot, and encourage child to explore it while you are there.*

- *find a building with many steps and let her practise.*

- *if you have a climbable tree in your garden or in a nearby park, encourage your four-year-old child to climb it. If you feel worried about possible accidents you could mutually agree on a height limit so that the child will not climb beyond that point.*

THE BODY: DANCING AND MOVEMENT

Play music frequently. If you cannot play an instrument yourself, sing — children are totally non-judgemental towards your actual singing talent, accepting you just as you are.

Music is expressed creativity, inviting our bodies to join in its game. Children love music. They grew into this world with a veritable orchestra playing inside the womb: the rumbling of intestines, the beat of the heart, the vibration of the voice-box. Play your favourite records so that your child gets plenty of opportunity to move to the rhythm if she wishes. Some days you can dance together.

Music suggests movements such as *galloping, skipping, marching, running, trotting, twisting, turning, hopping, leaping, tip-toeing, sliding, gliding, swaying,* and more.

These movements can all be carried out

- *fast and slow (gradually faster and slower)*

- *loud and soft (gradually louder and softer)*

- *high and low (gradually higher and lower).*

Show the child how to do these movements from time to time.

Skipping together hand in hand down the street or along a beach is such a liberating and fun thing to do!

Also suggest to the child to move like

- *an animal (mention the type of animal)*

- *the wind*

- *trees*

- *the seed growing into a flower*

- *the caterpillar turning into a butterfly*

- *a person with a limp*

- *a tall thing*

- *a short thing*

The child can also:

pop, sway, float, roll, ooze, melt,

wither, slither, bubble slide, rock,

float, stretch, and squirm.

Ask child to try to move from high on

body or in space, from her middle,

and from down low.

Finger Rhymes

I HAVE 10 LITTLE FINGERS

I have 10 little fingers (*show 10 fingers*),
They all belong to me (*point to self*),
I can make them do things (*wriggle fingers*),
Would you like to see?
I can open them up wide (*spread fingers*),
I can shut them up tight (*make fists*),
I can put them together (*hands together, as if praying*),
And make them hide (*hide behind back*).
I can jump them up high (*stretch hands above head*),
I can make them crouch low (*lower to floor*),
I can fold them quietly (*fold hands*),
And sit just so (*sit still*).

OPEN, SHUT THEM

Open, shut them (*open hands, and make fists*),
Open, shut them (*repeat above*),
Give a little clap (*clap hands*),
Open, shut them,
Open, shut them,
Lay them in your lap (*place hands in lap, and fold*).
Creep them, creep them,
Creep them, creep them (*creep fingers slowly from knee up . . .*),
Right up to your chin (*. . . to chin*),
Open wide your little mouth (*open mouth wide*),
But do not let them in (*quickly run fingers away behind back*).

THIS IS MY RIGHT HAND

This is my right hand (*hold up right hand*),
I'll hold it up high.
This is my left hand (*show left hand*),
I'll touch the sky (*raise left hand high above head*).
Right hand (*show right hand*),
Left hand (*show left hand*),
Roll them around (*roll hands around one another*),
Left hand (*hold up left hand*)
Right hand (*hold up right hand*),
Pound, pound, pound (*pound fists together*).

Body Naming Games

NOSE NOSE

Nose, nose, jolly red nose,
And what gave you that jolly red nose?
Nutmegs and ginger, spices and cloves,
That's what gave me this jolly red nose.

LITTLE GIRL WITH A CURL

There was a little girl and she had a little curl (*point to forehead*)
Right in the middle of her forehead.
And when she was good she was very very good (*smile sweetly*)
But when she was bad she was HORRID! (*make an ugly face*).

THESE ARE BABY'S FINGERS

These are X's (*child's name*) fingers, (*touch fingers*).
These are X's toes (*touch toes*),
This is X's tummy button (*touch belly button*),
Round and round it goes (*draw circles on his stomach*).

LET'S TAP OUR LEGS TOGETHER

Let's tap our legs together (*do actions the words suggest in this game*),
Let's tap our legs together,
Let's tap our legs together,
Because it's fun to do.
(*Create a beat with the words, as if it had music. You and your child can think up other body actions such as Let's . . . tap the floor, clap our hands, touch our noses, wriggle our ears, blink our eyes, twirl around . . . together*).

ONE IS A GIANT

One is a giant who stomps his feet
(stamp feet around room),
Two is a fairy so light and neat
(tippy-toe lightly around, arms flying),
Three is a mouse that crouches small
(crouch, make self small),
And four is a great big bouncing ball
(jump up and down, clapping).

CLAP YOUR HANDS

Clap, clap, clap your hands as slowly as you can.
Clap, clap, clap your hands as quickly as you can.
Shake, shake, shake your hands . . .
Roll, roll, roll your hands . . .
Rub, rub, rub your hands . . .
Wriggle, wriggle, wriggle your fingers . . .
Pound, pound, pound your fists . . .
Kick, kick, kick your feet . . .
Shrug, shrug, shrug your shoulders . . .
Dance, dance, dance your belly . . .
(Plus any other movements you can think of.)

SANDPLAY AND MUD HOLES

Sand is an excellent medium for child's play, as good a learning experience as waterplay. Compared to sophisticated toys on the market which are often limited to certain actions, sand is a really cheap and versatile addition to your outside play gym (see p. 101).

You can leave it in a pile or buy a small moulded wading pool to put it into. Cover the sand at night against cats and insects with a tarpaulin secured with bricks or rocks. Offer your child the following materials for sandplay:

- empty containers
- colander
- sieve
- funnels of different sizes
- wooden float from a hardware shop
- water/sand wheel from a toy supplier
- plastic cars or trucks
- sand or biscuit moulds
- water
- spades
- old saucepans
- wooden and other spoons
- plastic farm animals
- kitchen scales

Or

Dig a hole in the ground and let the hose trickle water into it — it will soon be a great mud hole. Provide the same materials as for sandplay.

Or

Make some *Mix and Mess* (see p. 59).

Movement Games

TEDDY BEAR, TEDDY BEAR

Teddy bear, teddy bear *(sit on floor, clap hands on 'teddy')*,
Turn around *(spin around on bottom)*,
Teddy bear, teddy bear *(clap hands twice)*,
Touch the ground *(tap floor)*.
Teddy bear, teddy bear *(clap hands twice)*,
Shine your shoes *(polish shoes with hands)*.
Teddy bear, teddy bear *(clap hands twice)*,
That will do *(cross arms firmly)*.

'How can children play without getting dirty?'

George Dennison, Author of 'Lives Of Children'

CATCHING AND THROWING

Use a balloon when playing this game with a younger child.

Method

Cup child's hands together in front of her, and prompt her to 'catch the ball'. You then throw the ball softly into her cupped hands, cheering if the ball stays put.

The child throws the ball back to you with both hands. Initially stand very close to child, then as the child starts to actively catch the ball, move further away.

Variation

Show child how to throw ball against wall, catching it as it comes back. This is a game the child can play alone, too.

Or

Child can throw up ball into the air above, and catch again.

UNDERARM

For both under- and overarm use a small soft ball that the child can hold one handed.

Method

Confirm child's preferred hand. Stand alongside child opposite a wall. Swing child's arm backwards gently, so that her arm is behind her, then guide the stiff arm forwards.

Ask child to hold a soft ball, and repeat the movement.

When arm comes forward, say 'Let go!' and the ball will bounce onto the wall and return to child.

Repeat until you feel that the child is able to do it alone.

Ask her to throw it to you underarm. Throw it back the same way, and catch with both hands.

OVERARM

Method

Stand facing an open door, alongside child, next to her preferred arm. Lift her arm up and slightly backwards. Ask her to make her arm stiff.

Holding a soft ball, repeat movement. When arm is up and slightly bent back, say 'Let go!', guiding her hand quickly straight over her head. Ball will go through door.

Repeat until you feel that the child is able to do it alone.

Ask her to throw the ball to you overarm — you can stand on the other side of the door opening. Throw it back to her, and prompt her to catch it with both hands.

Variation

Draw a circle about a head higher than child on outside wall, or on a piece of cardboard which can be hung on a closed door. Encourage child to hit the circle, using overarm.

Or

Buy a basketball ring and fix to outside of house. The height of the ring should be as high as child's hand stretched over her head when she stands on tiptoes. Let child throw ball into ring.

KICKING GAMES

Use a balloon with a younger child. Follow up with a very soft (foam) ball, and gradually end up with a tougher ball.

Kick to Each Other

Method

Stand about 2 m away from child, facing each other.

Kick the ball to his feet. Use kicks which push the ball along the ground rather than upwards.

Prompt child to return the kick.

Goal Kicking

Use a cardboard box placed against the wall for the goal — child can decorate it before use.

Chalk Goal

Draw a goal with chalk on the wall outside. If you have painted blackboard paint on a door or wall, you can draw on that and use it as the goal.

Variation

Draw a high goal on the wall for the skilled kicker. The child can kick up into the goal.

Door Goal

Use an open door as the goal.

BEANBAGS

Texture is excellent for children to practice catching and throwing.

Materials
dry beans
two pieces of 15 x 15 cm fabric (try two different textures such as corduroy and cotton)

Method

Sew fabric together securely on three sides.

Three-quarter fill with beans.

Sew last side securely.

The Game

Use beanbags for throwing, catching, tossing into basketball ring, and for target practice.

NB Do not use whole dried peas — children tend to roll them into inaccessible holes in their bodies!

PUNCHING JOE

An activity involving coordination of eye-hand-body movements.

Materials
old white sheet
felt pen
brushes
fabric paints
solvent
sewing machine
stuffing
rope

Method

Fold sheet in half. Ask child to lie on it with arms tightly at sides, trace around her with a felt pen being careful not to mark clothes.

The child can paint on eyes, hair and other features or they can cover the shape with their own hand or feet prints or any other method may be used to print inside the shape of her body.

KICK AND CATCH

Take turns to kick ball to one another, holding out hands to catch.

Left: Make beanbag in bright primary colours, or any left-over material.

Cut out front and back (fabric is folded and pinned together).
Sew most of Punching Joe together and stuff firmly.
Sew up the rest securely. Attach a handle onto head of Joe very firmly, and hang with nylon rope from a doorway or a tree, so that Joe is level with child, but slightly off the ground.

The Game

Child is encouraged to push Punching Joe around for both the exercise and eye-hand coordination practice, it also may be a way to release some aggression. Encourage the child to make sounds with each push.

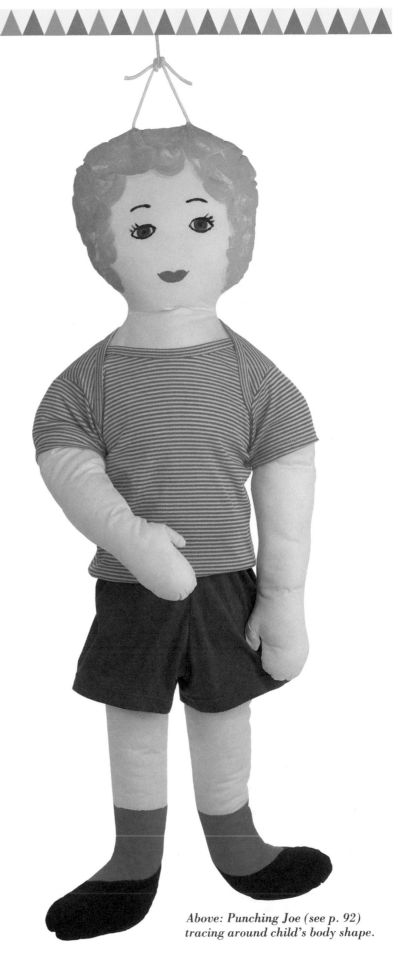

Above: Punching Joe (see p. 92)
tracing around child's body shape.

PEGGING OUT CLOTHES

Pinching open the pegs involves fine finger manipulation.

Materials

nylon clothes line
basin of tepid, soapy water
doll's clothing/other
pegs

Method

Stretch out a short clothes line at child's height near your own line.

Give child a basin with bubbly, tepid water and a few doll's clothes.

Place a number of pegs nearby.

Show child slowly how a peg opens and closes, and how to peg out clothes.

Child washes clothes and pegs them out.

Repeat several times — children love this activity.

WINDOW CLEANING

Offer this activity to your child just before you are ready to clean your windows.

Materials

window cleaner/scraper
soapy warm water

Method

Child wets glass, then uses scraper to wipe water away.

WALKING AND BALANCING GAMES

An activity for large muscle movements.
(*see also Hopscotch on p. 63.*)

FOLLOW THE TRACK

Materials

oil paint
turps
soap
water
cold cream

Method

If you have a concrete area, paint your child's feet with oil paint and guide him along, painting the feet again as needed.

Clean up child with turps and soap and water. Apply cold cream to feet. Allow paint to dry.

Using different colours, paint child's hands and ask him to make handprints in front of footprints, on the side of footprints, touching footprints, far from footprints, on top of footprints.

Clean child as above.

Allow paint to dry.

The Game

Encourage child to walk along his own footprints, and also to move on all fours, matching hands with handprints, feet with footprints.

Variation

If you haven't got any concreted area, or if you prefer a less permanent game, you can use leftover white sheet and fabric paints from Punching Joe *and follow same procedure as above for printing.*

Allow to dry.

Roll out and secure ends with beanbags. Child balances along as in the game above.

Or

Make footpaint (see Recipe for Paint and Paste, *p. 70) in two colours — choose two which may make a third, such as blue and yellow, or red and yellow.*

Cool paint and place in baking trays, one for each colour.

Roll out a long paper roll and secure with beanbags or rocks.

Variation

Try a squiggly line and a zigzaggy line. Think up other challenges.

The Game

Hold child's hand and encourage to step in both paints, one foot in each. Then slowly walk her along paper. Paint is slippery, so this game is also a balancing game, and she needs someone to hold her hand firmly. Walk her back to baking trays for another turn.

Better still, wait for another adult to hold her other hand, and pull her sliding along the length of paper. Try it yourself — it's fun!

End game at the end of the paper roll in a bucket of warm soapy water. Towel child dry.

LINE WALKING

An important activity for balance and awareness of their body in space.

Method

Chalk a straight line. Explain to child that all around the line is water, and he must walk on the line only.

Lead him along at normal walking pace.

Lead him along with one foot directly in front of the other.

Lead him along walking sideways.

Lead him along backwards.

OBSTACLE COURSE

Create an obstacle course for your child by plotting out a course for her to follow, thinking of things which will be challenging for her to try out along the way.

Use cardboard signs with bold numbers from 1 to 5 (1 to 10 for older children) to follow.

Materials

trampoline or old cot mattress for bouncing on/across
3 old tyres tied together for going through
boxes for going inside/over
a hill for going around/over
chairs, tables, hoops, stairs, ropes and so on

Example

Place three chairs in a row, with different heights for walking over.

Follow this with a table draped with a large cloth for climbing through.

Drape a string on the ground from table to balance on (or along).

Hang a hoop from a tree and place beanbags there to throw through.

Tie a string 15 cm above ground between two chairs to crawl under and jump over.

Draw two chalk lines on paved path for child to walk between.

CONCEPTS

When setting up obstacle course think of having your child experience with his body the following concepts which also help cement knowledge for reading/writing: *under, over, through, across, below, above, line, around, straight, curved, short, tall, slanted, top, middle, bottom.*

PAINTING WITH WATER

Materials

small (paint-type) bucket
water
approximately 70 cm string
pastry brush (or 'real' paintbrush)

Method

Half-fill bucket with water, and tie brush to handle.

Encourage child to paint exterior wall, path, trees, fence, and more.

TIN STILTS

It's fun learning to master how to balance on stilts.

Materials
2 empty 825 g cans
hammer
oil-based house paint
large screwdriver
nylon string

Method

De-label cans and hammer rough edges smooth.

Paint cans in bright colours (with two coats if necessary).

Using screwdriver, hammer a hole near bottom of can and hammer another hole diagonally across from first hole.

Pull nylon string through.

Stand can upside down, and stand child on it.

Measure string so that it reaches up to child's fingers as they bend up in order to hold it.

Cut string and tie firmly inside can.

The Game

Child stands on both cans holding on to the string and attempts to walk.

While balancing and walking on stilts the child needs to be very aware of where he is in relation to the space around him.

BALANCE WALK

Exploring a familiar street walk in a new way.

Method

Pick a day when you have plenty of time, and tell child that you and she are going to go for a walk to find things she can walk and balance along.

Holding her hand, walk her along suitable low brick garden fences, along cracks in the sidewalk and along fences which rise and fall according to the slant of the street.

JUMPING GAME

Jumping and balancing involves the control of large muscle movement.

Materials
2 chalked circles on ground

Method

Hold child's hands and stand opposite him in one circle.

On the count of three jump together into other circle.

On the count of three jump together into first circle.

BOAT

Materials
triangular fabric
glue
15 cm dowel
block of pine wood

Method

Prepare two consecutive holes on one side of fabric.

Child glues dowel onto wood and fits dowel through fabric through holes.

It sails, too!

WOODWORK

Allow child to explore hammering. Child can hold flat-headed nail in place with pliers — this saves fingers and tears — while hammering.

Also provide woodwork glue and assorted interesting items for pasting: leather, fabric, corks, coloured paper, smaller bits of wood. Most timber yards have free scrap bits of wood which are just the right size for woodwork. Pine is a soft and suitable wood to work with.

SCREWDRIVING

An activity for the older child because of the fine twisting movement of the wrist.

Materials
- short screwdriver
- short screws
- thick nail
- block of pine wood

Method

Show child how to keep screwing the same way in order to get screw down into wood.

Start the child off until screw gets stuck in wood.

It helps to hammer a thick nail a little way into wood first, and then remove nail before screwing screw into hole. Child will be fascinated with this activity, and feel privileged to be allowed to work with these items.

Above: An example of the types of materials that may be used to create a face on wood.

FACE

A strong glue is needed to glue onto wood.

Materials
- scissors
- wood
- bits of cardboard
- leather
- hammer
- flat-headed nails
- block of pine wood

Method

Child cuts out shapes for eyes, nose, mouth, or as desired, from cardboard, leather or fabric, or use small pieces of wood as facial features and hammers these onto block of wood to make a face. Glue may be used instead of nails.

BOWLING

Game involves skills in control of large muscle movement and eye-hand coordination.

Materials

collection of 1 litre plastic bottles*, partly filled with sand or water
chalk
large firm ball

Method

Draw a circle for child to stand in, and about 1.5 m away trace bottle bottoms in a straight line, or in bowling shaped triangle if you have 10 bottles.

Stand bottles in their shapes; child stands in his circle and rolls ball towards bottles.

Child replaces bottles into drawn outlines, and rolls ball again.

* Bottles can be decorated by child with vinyl paints.

GEOMETRIC ART

Mark the wooden board with pencil spots for the child to use as a guide when hammering in the nails.

Materials

flat-headed nails
block of pine wood
hammer
coloured elastic bands

Method

Child hammers nails into wood (not right down), and stretches elastic bands between nails to make interesting geometric patterns.

TARGET

Distance from the target will alter the difficulty of hitting the 'bullseye'.

Materials

cardboard
red and black paint
single hole punch
string

Method

Paint large red circle on cardboard. Inside this paint a smaller circle. If you can fit it, paint another circle inside the two others. In the centre paint a black round dot for 'bullseye'.

Punch two holes 10 cm apart at the top of board (measure just to make sure) and thread string through. The target is now ready to hang for the game of aiming and throwing small beanbags or a tennis ball into the bullseye.

RING TOSSES (QUOITS)

If you haven't any quoits, cut out centre of small paper or plastic plates and place a stick in the ground, so it stands up straight about 20 cm out of the ground.

Child stands close and tosses homemade quoits similarly to frisbees in the direction of the stick (the tossing is done with a flick of the wrist, the ring held horizontally).

The idea of the game is to land the quoits over the stick.

BALANCING ACT

Developing an appreciation of space in relation to the child's own body size and shape.

Method

Encourage child to walk, with outstretched right arm, to a short distance while holding an item in her flat hand, palm up.

Next, encourage child to repeat with an item in her left hand.

Try the same with something on her head, walking slowly and then walking fast.

Add another item on top of the one on the head.

Try all items at once.

Take turns, and have a laugh!

Below: Target could also be placed on the ground.

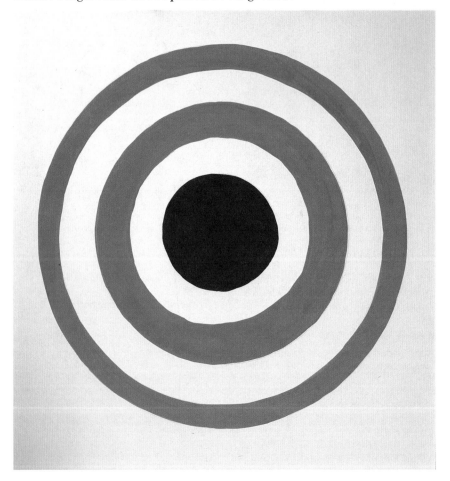

STRING AND BALL GAME

A game involving eye-hand coordination and learning to take turns.

Materials
old broomstick
knife
drill
tennis ball
1 m nylon rope
table tennis bats

Method

Sharpen one end of broomstick.

Drill a hole through other end, 5 cm from the top.

Drill a hole through middle of tennis ball, so that it goes through the other side.

Tie nylon rope through ball and make a big knot at bottom so it will not slip through.

Tie other end through hole in broomstick.

Hammer broomstick into ground and take turns to hit ball with bats, standing opposite one another.

FRISBEE

An activity for the older child; to fly the frisbee may need a bit of practice.

Method

Use a frisbee or a used disposable plastic plate (which the child can decorate) to toss around the garden or in the park.

Show child how to hold plate horizontally, then swing bent arm from chest straight out in front of body.

Let go of frisbee when the arm is extended out to one side.

Child can experiment to find movements which suit him.

GARDEN PLAY GYM

In tackling this activity skills in problem solving are explored.

Pulleys

Materials
2 single pulleys from hardware store
rope to fit
child's bucket

Method

Fix one pulley to side of tree or other tall place at child's height.

Fit other pulley to another tree close by. Feed rope through both pulleys and tie a knot. Tie bucket to rope. Child can now transport bucket by pulling rope.

Work out a game with child so that the pulley game has some purpose — for instance, create a platform for bucket to deliver sand to.

Bar Swing

Suitable for older children; an activity for large and small muscle development.

Materials
saw
broomstick
drill
2 lengths of nylon string (washing line thickness)

Method

Saw approximately 60 cm off broomstick and drill a hole around 5 cm in from each end.

Feed nylon string through both holes and tie securely, using a number of knots.

Tie other ends to good tree branch or through an eye-screw into door frame. Height should be reachable by tip-toeing child.

SKIPPING

For the older child; practicing eye-hand-foot coordination and balance.

Method

Use a heavy rope to tie on to a pole, or some other permanent fixture.

Swing the rope for the child. Use a skipping-chant.

ROPE LADDER

Expanding the Bar Swing (p.101) activity.

Method

Use Bar Swing *materials and method, making the bars 40 cm long for each rung.*

Secure each rung before adding next one, leaving approximately 25 cm between each new rung.

Hang as above, with bottom rung one step up from child.

Variation

Use slats instead of round rungs.

STEAM BOAT TYRE

This swing can also be built without the base.

Materials

1 tyre
plastic coated wire
wooden board
saw
nylon rope
stanley knife

Method

Make 4 holes — evenly spaced on the inside of the tyre.

Thread coated wire through and knot securely.

Slip wooden board on top of wire. The board will need to be cut to fit inside the tyre without much movement.

Make 3 holes — evenly spaced — on upper side of tyre. Attach nylon rope and hang on branch.

Attach another piece of rope further away so the child can use this to swing themselves.

TYRE SWING

Materials

1 tyre textile radial (not steel belted)
chalk
stanley knife
nylon rope

Method

Draw chalk lines on the tyre to indicate where you are to cut (see photographs).

Cut away steel bands on tyre. Then cut away two–thirds of the tread, leaving a band 40—50 mm wide on both sides.

Turn the tyre inside out and hang with two ropes.

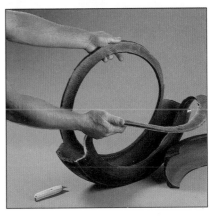

RED LIGHT

This is a really exciting game, which helps to perfect excellence of movement.

Method

Person who is 'in' stands close to, and facing, the wall.

Others who are not 'in' stand at opposite end of room, or, if the game is played outside, at some pre-arranged spot.

People who are not 'in' move silently forward.

As soon as 'in' person turns around — and this can be at any time and with any frequency — others must freeze. If anyone is caught moving, they have to go back to the starting point again. 'In' person then turns back to wall and others are free to move forward.

When one person reaches the wall without being discovered or disqualified, he shouts 'Red Light' and is now the new 'in' person.

Everyone starts again.

Variation

The ending is different: when the first person reaches 'in' person, he is tapped and has to chase her back to the start. If she is caught, she has to start again, but if not she becomes the next person to be 'in'.

BOUNCING

Developing large muscle coordination and control.

Method

Using a bouncy ball, bounce gently with your outstretched hand held over it, ready to push down again.

Then stand alongside child with your hand over hers, bouncing the ball.

Prompt child to try it herself.

Variation

Child can put outstretched hands directly next to each other in order to use hands as a bat, and can bounce ball 'overhand' onto wall.

To help child, draw a circle on the wall at child's mouth-level.

Or

Using a table tennis bat, child can hit ball against the wall and attempt to hit subsequent returning balls.

Or

Pierce a hole through a table tennis ball. Lead a 50 cm piece of string through holes and tie knot. Now tie the ball to a table tennis bat and

encourage child to bounce it on the floor or up in the air.

FOLLOW UP FOR BODY SKILLS ACTIVITIES

- *riding tricycles, bikes, scooters (why not make large cardboard traffic signs and a pedestrian crossing out the back one day?)*
- *swimming*
- *horse riding*
- *ballet*
- *gymnastics*
- *roller-skating*
- *ski-ing*
- *tennis*
- *table tennis*
- *soccer*
- *ice-skating*
- *rowing*
- *hockey*
- *baseball*
- *bowls*
- *cricket*
- *basketball*
- *netball*

LEARNING TO LACE

One point all teachers agree upon is that a school-aged child should have certain self-help skills, such as getting dressed. The most difficult one of these is the tying of shoelaces.

LACING

Threading and sewing are good preliminary activities to lacing.

Materials

magazines
scissors
paste
firm cardboard
clear self-adhesive plastic
wad punch
long shoelaces (boot laces)

Method

Cut out a picture that your child likes and glue onto cardboard.

Cover with self-adhesive plastic and punch holes along edge, 4 cm apart.

Tie shoelace onto first hole, and show child how to lace in and out, like sewing.

Variation

Trace around child's shoe onto red cardboard.

Cover with clear self-adhesive plastic.

Punch holes along centre, two in each row, 4 cm apart, so that there are five rows altogether.

Start the lacing, showing child how to do it as on a shoe. Do not show any other aspect of the skill at this stage. Child can do this activity from time to time.

OLD SHOE PUZZLE

Materials

old lace-up shoe
scissors
skewer
firm cardboard
darning (or raffia) needle
wool

Method

Cut off top section of old shoe (the flaps on both sides which have the lacing).

Skewer holes into cardboard at 1 cm intervals. Punch matching holes around falps of old shoe and sew onto cardboard. Child can use this puzzle to practise lacing.

KNOTTING

Materials

long piece of string or strips of fabric or very thick wool

Method

Child ties plain knots (same as first knot tied in a shoelace) over and over, starting in the centre of 1 m long string or wool.

Finish activity when the string is used up, or when child is tired.

Use as a bookmark or belt.

Rhyme

There was an old woman who lived in a shoe
She had so many children she didn't know what to do.
So she gave them some broth without any bread
She whipped them all soundly and sent them to bed.

LACING DADDY'S SHOES

Method

When the child can lace through holes reasonably, bring out a few pairs of tennis shoes, dad's shoes or old school shoes.

Have child practise, including the first knot.

TYING THE BOW

Method

Using a real shoe, explain to the child to make two loops. Show how this is done. Show how to take one loop behind the other while holding both. Then bring the loop forward and through newly created third loop. Pull both firmly to tie.

Do each action very slowly, holding one shoe in your hand, while child follows each action with a shoe of her own.

The joy of achievement is worth the effort. But you will be tying many shoelaces until then — most children do not learn this skill before the age of four or five.

Home Activities

The activities have been listed with recommended ages. These are only suggested ages, you will find that your child could benefit from the activity earlier, and most certainly the older child can benefit, practice skills and gain pleasure from the same activity.

	12 MONTHS	2 YEARS	3 YEARS	4 YEARS	5 YEARS
READING		baby's own book, alphabet biscuits, rhyming games, TV viewing	necklace threading, alphabet soup, most important words, tell me a story, dice game, make-a-book, labelling, talking games, what's that sign	taping stories, alphabet bingo, word bingo, listening skills game, sound hunt, match sounds, memory games, cloud shapes, sentence maker, movement cards	reading machine, word scramble
WRITING	feely blanket, shape box	dressing up, feely cards	bottle/jar-top box, feely letters, sewing into sponges, feely sticks, eye-dropper experiment, cooking activities	lock board, sewing into card, draw a picture, tracing	film strip bookmarks, weaving, be a letter
MATHEMATICS		water-level cans, play dough	maths by cooking, puzzles, colour puzzles, mix and mess (3+), sorting (3+)	time, dough numbers, dots-to-numbers-bingo, what's the time Mr Wolf?, marble game, quantity game (4+)	hopscotch, domino, sorting sets, scrambled numbers, weighing game, all number bingo, geometric shape drawing, operation game, water level game, neighbourhood map, how long is 100 (5+), calculator game (5+), multiplication bingo (5+)
ART		collage, wool and fabric, block stamps, lemon and apple printing, potato printing	cutting and pasting, foil/cellophane painting, dyed serviettes (3+), tissue strips (3+), sugared chalk (3+), cottonbud, painting (3+), crayon/wax and water paint (3+), punching (holes) (3+), cards for special days (3+)	masking tape painting, pizza pictures, glue printing, rubbing, cellophane and tissue strips, wet paper painting, kite, decorated milk cartons	doilies, animal templates, textured animal shapes
PHYSICAL AGILITY	rolling games, balloon play, finger rhymes, body naming games, tyre swing	catch the bubbles, climbing, body: dancing and movement, sandplay and mud holes, catching and throwing, bean bags, painting with water (2+), steam boat swing	underarm (3+), overarm (3+), kicking games, punching Joe, pegging out clothes, window cleaning, walking and balancing games, line walking, obstacle course, tin stilts (3+), balance walk, jumping gym	kick and catch, woodwork, face, bowling, ring tosses, balancing act, target, garden play gym, rope ladder, red light	screwdriving, geometric art, string and ball game, frisbee, skipping, lacing, old shoe puzzle, knotting, lacing daddy's shoes

Foundation Handwriting

A B C D E F G H I
J K L M N O P Q R
S T U V W X Y Z

a b c d e f g h i
j k l m n o p q r
s t u v w x y z
1 2 3 4 5 6 7 8 9 0

Index

A

accidents 12
addition (mathematics) 66
age appropriateness for activities 13
aggression 93
agility *see* fine motor skills physical agility
alphabet *see* letters
anger 93
animal shape, textured 83
animal templates 83
apple printing 76
arithmetic 66, 69
art 70–85
    see also drawing, painting, printing
authoritarian parenting 10–11

B

"Baby's Own Book" 20–21
balancing games 94–95, 97, 100
balloon play 86
bar swing 101
bathplay 52
beanbags 91
bingo
    alphabet 26–27
    dots-to-numbers 60–61
    multiplication 69
    numbers 65
    word 27
biscuits
    alphabet 22
    geometric shape 56
blackboards 42
blanket, tactile 40
blindfold game 61
block stamps 75
boat 97
body naming rhymes 89
body skills 86–105
bookmarks, making 49
books 18–19
    see also reading
    baby's own 20–21
    making 30
    reading from 31
bottle-top box 44
bouncing game 104
bowling 99
bows, tying 107
brain 6
brushes, paint 73
bubbles, catching game 88
butter, make-our-own 49

C

calculator games 68
capital letters 38

cardboard for artwork, size of 72
cards
    see also flashcards
    "feely" 44
    for special days 79
"Catch the bubbles" game 88
catching 91–92
cellophane
    and tissue strips 81
    painting on 75
chalk, sugared 78
chocolate
    biscuits 56
    ice-cream 56
climbing 88
cloud shapes 34
collage 74–75, 78, 81
colour
    experimentation 73–74
    problems 12
    puzzle 58
    readiness 12
coloured sand, sawdust and wood shavings 72
comics 16
concrete for writing on 43
cooking
    fine motor skills 48
    learning mathematics 55–57
    learning reading 22, 24
cottonbud painting 78
crayons 43
    water-paint 79
curiosity 12
cursive script 38
cutting
    and pasting 75
    lines 75

D

dancing 88
days of the week 62
dice game 30
directional parenting 11
discipline 10–11
display of child's works 14
division (mathematics) 66
doilies 82
domino 63
dot to dot shapes game 63
dots-to-numbers bingo 60–61
dough 54–55
    numbers 60
dramatic activities 18
drawing 51
    geometric shapes 65
dressing up 41
duration of activities 14
dyes 70

macaroni and rice 72
    sand, sawdust and wood shavings 72
    serviettes 78

E

easels 72
encouragement 10
    art 73–74
expectations of parents 10, 73–74
experimentation, role of 6, 7, 86
eye-dropper experiment 47
eye–hand coordination 40–41, 47–50, 86

F

face, woodwork 98
feel *see* tactile surfaces
film strip bookmarks 49
fine motor skills 40, 47
finger rhymes 89
flashcards
    important words 25
    reading from a book 31
foil painting 75
"Follow the track" game 94–95
foundation script 109
frisbee 101
fruit salad 48

G

garden play gym 101
geometric shapes
    biscuits 56
    drawing 65
    understanding 54
    woodwork 98
glue 70
    see also paste
    printing 80
greeting card jigsaw 58
gross motor ability 86–105
guilty parent syndrome 15
gym 101

H

handedness 38
home activities 108
hopscotch 63
"How long is 100" game 68

I

ice-cream 56
icing 22, 56
interview 32

USEFUL INFORMATION

WEIGHTS AND MEASURES

In this book, metric measures and their imperial equivalents have been rounded out to the nearest figure that is easy to use. Different charts from different authorities vary slightly.

LENGTH

Metric	Imperial
5 mm	¼ in
1 cm	½ in
2 cm	¾ in
5 cm	2 in
8 cm	3 in
10 cm	4 in
12 cm	5 in
15 cm	6 in
20 cm	8 in
25 cm	10 in
30 cm	12 in
46 cm	18 in
50 cm	20 in
61 cm	24 in

DRY MEASURES

Metric	Imperial
15 g	½ oz
30 g	1 oz
45 g	1½ oz
60 g	2 oz
75 g	2½ oz
100 g	3½ oz
125 g	4 oz
155 g	5 oz
185 g	6 oz
200 g	6½ oz
250 g	8 oz
300 g	9½ oz
350 g	11 oz
375 g	12 oz
400 g	12½ oz
425 g	13½ oz
440 g	14 oz
470 g	15 oz
500 g	1 lb (16 oz)
750 g	1 lb 8 oz
1 kg	2 lb

LIQUIDS

Metric	Imperial
30 mL	1 fl oz
60 mL	2 fl oz
100 mL	3½ fl oz
125 mL	4 fl oz (½ cup)
155 mL	5 fl oz
170 mL	5½ fl oz (⅔ cup)
200 mL	6½ fl oz
250 mL	8 fl oz (1 cup)
300 mL	9½ fl oz
375 mL	12 fl oz
410 mL	13 fl oz
470 mL	15 fl oz
500 mL	16 fl oz (2 cups)
600 mL	1 pt (20 fl oz)
750 mL	1 pt 5 fl oz (3 cups)
1 litre	1 pt 12 fl oz (4 cups)
(1000 mL)	